D1265027

Comparative Literature

CONCEPTS OF LITERATURE

GENERAL EDITOR: WILLIAM RIGHTER

Department of English
University of Warwick

Comparative Literature

Concepts of Literature

By Henry Gifford

Winterstoke Professor of English
University of Bristol

LONDON
ROUTLEDGE & KEGAN PAUL
NEW YORK: HUMANITIES PRESS

PN
871
G5
1969

First published in 1969
by Routledge & Kegan Paul Ltd
Broadway House, 68–74 Carter Lane
London E.C.4
Printed in Great Britain
by Willmer Brothers Limited
Birkenhead
© Henry Gifford 1969

SBN 7100 6372 5 (C)
SBN 7100 6377 6 (P)

General Editor's Introduction

The study of literature has normally centred on the consideration of work, author, or historical period. But increasingly there is a demand for a more analytic approach, for investigation and explanation of literary concepts of crucial ideas and issues—topics which are of general importance to the critical consideration of particular works. This series undertakes to provide a clear description and critical evaluation of such important ideas as 'symbolism', 'realism', 'style' and other terms used in literary discussion. It also undertakes to define the relationship of literature to other intellectual disciplines: anthropology, philosophy, psychology, etc., for it is in connection with such related fields that much important recent critical work has been done. *Concepts of Literature* will both account for the methodology of literary study, and will define its dimensions by reference to the many activities that throw light upon it. Individual works will describe the fundamental outlines of particular problems and explore the frontiers that they suggest. The series as a whole will provide a survey of recent literary thought.

While Professor Gifford sets out to describe the character and purpose of comparative literary studies in the broadest possible terms, the particular value of his approach lies in seeing such studies as the natural product of any effort to understand modern poetry and contemporary literary movements. He takes the work of Eliot and Pound to derive from a cosmopolitan literary sensibility drawing on the poetry of several languages and many centuries. The interpretation of such works requires a knowledge of the literatures on which it draws, and the modern reader or student is dependent, either directly or at second hand on comparative study. Among many questions Professor Gifford is especially concerned with the study of literature in translation, with the Transatlantic character of modern literary experience, and with the importance of finding a place for Comparative Literature in the university.

WILLIAM RIGHTER

Contents

decorum: the elegies of Machado and Hardy—*Le Cimetière marin* as a conclusive statement.

Foreword

'Comparative literature' cannot pretend to be a discipline on its own. I should rather define it as an area of interest —one that was proclaimed by Goethe when he predicted a *Weltliteratur* in which all the nations would have their voice. Goethe's intelligence—so free, insatiable and unconfined—sets the ideal for comparative study. One can ascertain from Fritz Strich (in *Goethe and World Literature*) the eager diversity of his reading. Arnold in our country was the pupil of Goethe; and it is their curiosity, their vision, that this book tries to recommend.

Its plan is easily understood from the Table of Contents. One or two chapters may, I suspect, need defending, or at any rate the reasons for their appearance. I begin with an account of the interest taken in literatures other than their own by certain writers of the twentieth century. The critic has often found himself indebted to poets and novelists for the sudden illuminations they give about their own work and that of others (often for them an inextricable concern); and I should wish the comparative student to acquire something of the imaginative boldness that characterizes the poet in this field. The next chapter, on the common tone shared by writers in a national tradition, serves, I hope, to indicate the kind of sensibility a reader ought to develop. I have written in the following chapter of Europe and its continuities not because comparative literature means Europe alone, but because here is a natural and significant field for the English critic, and one that demands particular study at this time, when European civilization as something distinct may be in its final stage.

Translation seemed worth looking at, since we must all depend on it to some extent in comparative work, and an awareness of its problems will help the student. I have discussed at fair length the question of comparative study in the university, both for undergraduates and postgraduates; and the special case of American literature is treated at the conclusion as pointing the need for adjustment to a new stage in the world's culture.

The comparatist works under all kinds of difficulty. He has to take many risks, and is more obviously prone to delusions than other critics. But when the study of any single literature today comes to resemble the nation's high-roads—a welter of traffic increasingly caught up in its own fumes—he can feel exhilaration in the open spaces before him, the large and generous vistas where so much is yet to be tried.

1

The education of a
modern poet

What I examine in this opening chapter is the remarkable
awareness of some twentieth-century writers that only a
world horizon will serve them. The exploration of foreign
literature, even at a good distance from their own, has
seemed a necessity of their being. Matthew Arnold required that 'every critic should try and possess one great
literature, at least, besides his own; and the more unlike
his own, the better' (Arnold, 1865, 39). This he felt was a
law of criticism; it appears in our day to be almost a law
of the creative imagination.

Our first example, Ezra Pound, is beyond any cavil a
learned poet, even if the learning can sometimes be exposed as superficial or wrong-headed. He seems to have
mistaken, with Fenollosa, the essential nature of the
Chinese written character; his misreadings of Propertius
are wanton; he played fast and loose with the Old English
of 'The Seafarer'. Yet more often than not his errors have
been fruitful. Any treatise on comparative literature would
have to mention Pound, the earlier the better. He figures
here, at the head of this chapter, for three reasons: first,
for the range of his achievement; second, for the power of
his influence; third, because he is an American.

To start with the final reason: an American writer, half

inside European culture and half outside, is born to comparisons. He shares a language that already houses one of
the world's richest literatures; but nothing ties him to our
tradition; he is no longer restricted by any Navigation
Acts of the mind. As Pound wrote of the Americans in
1914 with a heady enthusiasm: '... our opportunity is
greater than Leonardo's: we have more aliment, we have
not one classic tradition to revivify, we have China and
Egypt, and the unknown lands lying upon the roof of the
world—Khotan, Kara-shar and Kan-su' (Pound, 1954,
224). The American poet holds a position today that
fairly soon (whether we like it or not) could be the position of poets in older countries: while representing an extreme case, he is not untypical both in his restlessness and
his craving for order. Among American poets, none has
attempted so much as Pound. The *Cantos* are designed to
be the Great American Poem of modern times. They are
also meant as a contribution to world literature, a meeting of the waters.

Pound's interest moved from Victorian poetry (Browning
and the Pre-Raphaelites) to the Provençal and Italian
medieval writers he had studied at the University; he
reached backwards to Ovid, Propertius, Homer and
Sappho: and, with the help of Fenollosa's researches, to
the Japanese *haiku* and the *Noh* play and the Confucian
anthology. These are only his principal resting-points. We
should not dismiss such activity out of hand as proof that
he lacks a centre. Pound has been called a 'translation
poet'. This need not imply that all his light is derivative.
He has been concerned with seeking out and enlarging the
tradition—not merely of one literature, but of literature
in all places. He has called for 'a criticism of poetry based
on world-poetry, on the work of maximum excellence',
a criticism which must be done by those who 'have had
the tools in their hands' (ibid., 225). It will depend largely

on translation which elsewhere he has recognized as a form of criticism (ibid., 74). The practitioners must make available to their own public 'the work of maximum excellence', a process which has been going on through the ages, ever since the *Odyssey* was rendered for the Romans into Saturnian verse during the First Punic War.

Given his immense range, how much is Pound able to unify and control? We are assuming that the interests of Pound should weigh seriously with the modern reader; in effect, that an educated man (so far as literature goes) will need to follow Pound into these foreign literatures, so that they become a living part of his experience. Arnaut Daniel and Guido Cavalcanti do not come appreciably nearer, I think, in Pound's versions. He wanted to recover in Cavalcanti 'the radiant world where one thought cuts through another with clean edge, a world of moving energies...' (ibid., 154). But his actual renderings of Cavalcanti are mannered, awkwardly ninetyish for all their vigour. 'The Mediterranean sanity' he admired will have to be looked for in passages of the *Cantos* where Cavalcanti and the *Divine Comedy* are working at one remove, as a peculiarly clear atmosphere. It remains doubtful whether Pound has convinced the world that the Troubadours and Cavalcanti still count away from the lecture-room. Dante, on the other hand, partly through the attention given to his work by Pound and Eliot, has entered the modern consciousness, and all of him is potentially there, not simply the poet of Hell, as with the Victorians.

But perhaps the crucial question is that of Chinese and Japanese poetry. Nothing testifies more vividly to the opening of horizons than the way in which *Japonisme* came in, from the later nineteenth century. And it is not Gautier or the Goncourts or Whistler so much as Pound (though he learned from the others) who discovered the application of the Japanese example. Earl Miner has shown that Chinese thought (about ethics and history) and Japanese form (in poetry and drama) have each contributed very much to his development (Miner, 1958, 152). Pound the Imagist—that is to say, Pound the poet still in course of finding himself—recognized in the *haiku* or *hokku* (a Japanese poem of three lines arranged in five, seven and five syllables) a conception and a technique he could make his own. The conception was that of the 'natural object' as 'the proper and perfect symbol' (ibid., 124); the technique that of 'Super-Position', the setting of 'one idea ... on top of another' (ibid., 114). Pound gives an example from a Japanese *haiku*:

> The fallen blossom flies back to its branch :
> A butterfly.

(Machado has nearly this image:

> ... el blanco del almendro en la colina
> ¡oh nieve en flor y mariposa en arbol !
> *(Poesías completas*, 1943, 201.)

He uses this technique nowhere more finely than in the *Pisan Cantos*. Here is one example selected by Miner:

> did we ever get to the end of Doughty :
>   The Dawn in Britain?
>   perhaps not
>   (summons withdrawn, sir.)
> (bein' aliens in prohibited area)
> clouds lift their small mountains
>   before the elder hills
>   (Canto lxxxiii.)

The aliens are Yeats and Pound in wartime Sussex, and

the whole scene is evaluated in the light of its final image which reassures the poet that he, like the elder hills beyond his Pisan confinement, will survive the persecutions which (not surprisingly) came to him from a power he regards as illusory.

In the *Cantos* Pound took from the *Noh* plays 'what we call Unity of Image' (Miner, 140) as an organizing principle. They do not, obviously, like the *Noh* plays, cohere round a single image. There are three main image-fields, if we can so describe them, for the *Cantos*: Renaissance Italy, Adams's and Jefferson's America, and Chinese history. Each is presented with massive detail: the reader gets thorough instruction in all these periods. As the *Cantos* unfold we come to see that China can be made part of our experience no less than the worlds of Malatesta or President Adams. Eventually Chinese ideograms are planted like banners in the text, and we learn to recognize them. In this way Pound has admitted a new stream into Western poetry. The method may be peremptory, if not violent. Yet it enlarges our sensibility and compels a fresh understanding of the simplest ideas. He decided that Chinese thought can be located in Western poetry through the ideogram, an object like Sigismondo's temple which takes many lights in the poem but stands firm. Other approaches may be found as Chinese culture grows more familiar. It has at any rate moved up to the frontiers and perhaps over them.

Eliot demanded, in words often quoted from the best-known of his essays, that a poet should write 'not merely with his own generation in his bones, but with a feeling that the whole of the literature of Europe from Homer and within it the whole of the literature of his own country has a simultaneous existence and composes a simultaneous order' (Eliot, 1951, 14). Pound has extended the order to take in literatures outside Europe, but their idea is the same. An American has to define where he stands intellectually and imaginatively in relation to all other writing, in whatever tradition may be used. Miner distinguishes between the attitudes of the Americans and the English among the Imagists towards Japanese culture. Both learned a technique from its poetry; but whereas the English Imagists went no farther than this, the Americans needed to clarify what their discovery meant to American culture. They felt that the United States was called upon to unite East and West (Miner, 180). World literature is an easier concept for the American, accustomed to the mingling of races on his own soil.

Something like a world literature declares itself in the *Cantos*, which open with a recall of the *Odyssey* and the *Poema de mio Cid*, and have soon reached 'the pines at Takasago', 'Ecbatan, of plotted streets', and with it the beginnings of civilization:

> To North was Egypt,
>   the blue deep Nile
>   cutting low barren land,
> Old men and camels
>   working the water-wheels ..
>   (Canto v.)

Many of Pound's allusions are lost on the reader. But if the detail escapes him, the broad picture shines clearly enough. One poet at least has tried to encompass many of the moments in human civilization—he ignores the Hebraic stream—to show their meaning for one another, and to knit them together in a single consciousness. The *Cantos*, like *Finnegans Wake*, lay claim to a very large tract of recorded experience. Both works rely on a much more diversified learning than is attainable by all but the most unusual of readers. Yet, once having known these possibilities, literature will hardly retreat. What seems outlandish to one generation very soon, if it makes sense, becomes natural for its successor.

No doubt Pound's special kind of awareness belongs particularly to a literature still forming. Our own literature at the time of the Renaissance, or Russian literature in Pushkin's day, showed a similar desire for appropriation, though these had a much firmer native base than the American today. Pushkin ran through French poetry of his father's time and his own, through Byron, Shakespeare and Scott, he touched on Hafiz, Dante, the Koran and Bunyan, he refused nothing of interest that came to hand. Goethe, of course, provides the supreme example of a modern poet seeking to communicate with all literatures and to assimilate them all. The situation of Germany when he lived, still waiting for national unity and a German renaissance, made for a curiosity and receptiveness that are perhaps paralleled in our own situation now, when the idea of one intellectual world begins to be realized.

Such curiosity and receptiveness, if we turn to English literature, will be found in Arnold, of course, and (for a modern example) in Lawrence. As a poet Arnold made his cautious mark; as a critic he guided and in part reflected the taste of an educated public. His field was properly Europe, American literature being for him no more than a department, none too satisfactory, of his own. He was acquainted with English literature in some depth, the Greek and Roman classics, and the outstanding writers of France, Italy and modern Germany. Late in life he threw a glance towards Russian literature, which he encountered in Tolstoy's work, notably *Anna Karenina*. But if Arnold displays the comparative view at its best, though within obvious limits, we may find Lawrence today more appealing to our interest, more boldly affirmative. His faults of interpretation, his waywardness and obsessions deny him the large centrality of Arnold—if indeed such centrality can be won in an altered world. The value of Lawrence's explorations principally comes from the fact that he was driven to them by the necessities of his art. If we compare him as a critic, say, with his one-time friend, Middleton Murry, it is manifest that they both regarded literature in the same light. For each of them a given work meant self-discovery, a challenge to their own living. But Lawrence had more to discover and he met the challenge more ardently. The title Murry gave to a collection of his essays, *Countries of the Mind*, would never have been used by Lawrence. It implies a ruminative ease and a comfortably peripatetic habit quite alien to him. Lawrence's peculiar insight led him else-where: it revealed 'the spirit of place', a *foreignness* that the mind could see intuitively but not annex or accommodate.

Everything with Lawrence is a matter of living relation-ship. He explored more eagerly than most critics of his day, and struck through to the essentials as he found them. There are no half-hearted passages in his criticism, none of the evasiveness or superficiality that occasionally mars Eliot's writing. Lawrence prized in a critic like Sainte-Beuve 'the courage to admit what he feels, as well as the flexibility to *know* what he feels' (Lawrence, 1955, 119). He liked Sainte-Beuve for being '*emotionally* educated',* for his readiness to cope with each experience on its own terms. All the emphasis falls upon the par-ticular experience. Lawrence does not interest himself in arranging his perceptions, or in the kind of inquiry that stirs Eliot: What is a classic? What is minor poetry? And hence, where do we place George Herbert or Hopkins? The Sardinian writer Grazia Deledda may be a minor novelist. Lawrence recognizes that 'she is not a first-class

* Lawrence's italics.

genius', but she holds his attention, because of the community she describes. Grazia Deledda knows how 'to
create the passionate complex of a primitive populace'
(ibid., 292). And that suffices for him. Enough to render
truthfully his emotion in reading her novel. To classify,
to assign her a place in the European order, among 'the
existing monuments', does not concern him.

Lawrence had dealings with much that was best in
contemporary literature: with Hardy, perhaps the closest
of his predecessors; with Bennett, Galsworthy and Wells,
none of whom met his standards; he wrote on Tolstoy
and Dostoevsky, Rozanov and Shestov; on Thomas Mann
and Verga; and on the American classics of the nineteenth
century, to whom he gave a serious and probing attention
then almost unprecedented. And he had something to
say about new arrivals like Joyce, Forster, Dos Passos and
Hemingway. There is no great backward depth to his
view, and mostly not more than perfunctory and almost
jejune reference to the old masters. He cared for the
present and for so much of the past (Hardy, Tolstoy and
Dostoevsky, Cooper, Whitman, Melville) as had yet to
fulfil its meaning. Not all that signified in Europe seems
to have caught his eye; but he missed nothing, one would
guess, that might hold significance for himself.

Lawrence could be unjust, nagging and doctrinaire.
But he came to these works with a fierce passion of
inquiry. Thus the criticism he wrote, and equally the
novels and stories which respond to a challenge like that
of *Anna Karenina*, show all of them a single preoccupation. He divines immediately whether a book has the
emotional honesty, the truth to its occasion and place,
for which he is searching. And Lawrence goes out to
try conclusions with Melville or Dostoevsky, to grapple
with them and find what is genuine thew and sinew, and
what mere flabbiness. For him Europe and America

abound in opportunities, the Russian way of life, the Sicilian, the buried Etruscan, the surviving Hopi. There are no limits to his curiosity, and he speaks out:

European culture is a rootless thing in the Russians (ibid., 242).
    The trouble with Verga, as with all Italians, is that he never seems quite to know where he is (ibid., 272).
    ... it is perhaps easier to love America passionately, when you look at it through the wrong end of the telescope, across all the Atlantic water, as Cooper did so often, than when you are right there (ibid., 318).

These statements are uncompromising in their pungent candour. Lawrence puts forward each as showing a predicament. Whether he has told the complete truth may be argued. But the degree of his interest and sympathy allows him, as an experienced witness, to say these things.
    The essay on Verga's novel *Mastro-don Gesualdo* (ibid., 270–9) proves the quality of Lawrence as a critic—his range, exactitude, feeling for the particular, and sincerity. At the start he takes his bearings from *I Promessi Sposi*, 'one of the best and most interesting novels ever written', yet like the stories of Verga unaccountably neglected. He glances at Chekhov, in connection with *Cavalleria Rusticana*, then at Octave Feuillet and Gyp, and at Matilda Serao. All these references are needed to help define what Verga is, to bring out his artistic profile. Then Lawrence turns to the situation: 'Verga himself was a Sicilian, from one of the lonely agricultural villages in the south of the island'. And so to what he finds unsatisfactory in Verga: '... perhaps the gross vision of the man is not quite his own. All his movements are his own. But his main motive is borrowed'. So he proceeds to consider the pathetic power of *I Malavoglia* and to express quite simply 'the trouble with realism', as suffered

both by Verga and Flaubert, that the people of the story don't match up to the author's tragic conception. Finally, in the second half of the essay, he sets the Sicilian consciousness against the Russian, and he arrives at this view:

So that in *Mastro-don Gesualdo* you have the very antithesis of what you get in *The Brothers Karamazov*. Anything more un-Russian than Verga it would be hard to imagine: save Homer.

... [Gesualdo] has the energy, the quickness, the vividness of the Greek, the same vivid passion for wealth, the same ambition, the same lack of scruples, the same queer openness, without ever really openly committing himself.

... He puts no value on sentiment at all : or almost none : again a real Greek.

In all this Lawrence moves with the assurance of one who knows Europe and knows where to turn in its literature for the right comparisons. There are other novelists—Thomas Mann, for example—who possess a similar range. Lawrence's originality lies in his direct approach, and the boldness of his collocations. And, once again, everything is related to his central concern. In this way the poet, the working novelist, and occasionally the active critic deduce a pattern in Western literature, make clear the relations between contraries, sensitize and guide our experience.

Eliot has already been named in this chapter. As a critic he often expressed discomfort: he once complained that 'The creative artist in England finds himself compelled, or at least tempted, to spend much of his time and energy in criticism that he might reserve for the perfecting of his proper work: simply because there is no one else to do it' (Eliot, 1960, 46). The criticism which Eliot affected to write with his left hand, and which he read over again so unwillingly, came to dominate English and American minds for perhaps three decades. Like Pound, he had made himself free of the Old and the New Worlds, giving however his attention in the Old to Indian thought rather than to Chinese history and Japanese art. Like Lawrence, he turned eagerly to Europe, though one might almost say to a different Europe opening on the past, in which Dante and Virgil formed the centre of a beautifully scaled and ordered system. Eliot was fortunate in his education. He attended Harvard of 'the Golden Era', when Santayana, Royce, Babbitt, Kittredge were all to be heard, and he could gather ideas which would stay with him for a lifetime (Howarth, 1965, 64–94). Perhaps the most valuable thing Harvard gave him was an introduction to Dante. Ever since the time of Ticknor, nearly a hundred years before, Dante studies had been strong at Harvard, and teaching of the Romance literatures converged on them. Eliot's own poetry has kept Dante before its eyes from the very first. The wholeness he looked for—a union of intellect and feeling, of poetry, metaphysics, social thought and theology—he perceived in Dante, and it was in succession to Dante that he wanted to align his own poetry.

The idea of Europe, its medieval culture meeting in Dante, its modern culture still to be redeemed through his vision; the spiritual unity of Europe; its interdependence and variety and creative force; the civilizing energies of Europe—for all these Eliot cared as only perhaps an American, ill at ease with the twentieth century, could care. His review that he maintained from 1922 to 1939, *The Criterion*, tried to make Europe more fully conscious of itself. It owed something to the *Nouvelle Revue Française*, more perhaps to the New York *Dial* (ibid., 246), and throughout it reflected the interests of Eliot's own mind, his particular (somewhat narrow) understanding of Europe, his hopes for its revival. Eliot was attracted to the French intellect: to the ironic poetry of Corbière and Laforgue, but also to the extreme commitment of Baudelaire and Pascal which goes with a serenity of style. It was possible for him, where it might not have been for an English writer, to accept the characteristic French disciplines—imposed by the concern with form, the need to be definite even at the cost of a concealed simplification, the trust in method. Eliot remains, of course, essentially an American, but many of his preoccupations, and the expression of these, are French. His master in criticism at one time was Remy de Gourmont; his political ideas in large measure derived from Charles Maurras; his peculiar faith-in-doubt drew him to Pascal, whose desolation and painful ardour, scorn and humility are Eliot's own.

The imagination of a twentieth-century writer, if it is fair to generalize from three examples, two of them American, would appear to be synthetic. The American poets at least—Pound, Eliot, Stevens, Robert Lowell of the *Imitations*—seek to appropriate from sources hitherto foreign. They close the distances; theirs is a hospitable and a naturalizing poetry. And the Europeans are not far behind them: Rilke, possessed by his experience of Russia, then finding in Paris a 'severe and salutary discipline' which gave him the secret of form; Pasternak, who felt strong affinities with Rilke; Mandelstam, feeling the spell of Latin culture and also of the German language; Proust, powerfully attracted by Ruskin and George Eliot; Yeats, who could not reckon his debt to Catullus, Verlaine and Mallarmé, as revealed to him by Arthur Symons (Yeats, 1955, 319); Joyce with his wide and miscellaneous foraging. To understand any one of these writers it is not enough that you study their own literature. They compel the reader to look abroad and to live in more than one culture. They demand for their full appreciation the comparative sense.

Criticism at the present time needs to educate itself in the fashion of these poets and novelists. Already we have the example of Edmund Wilson—once more an American, prompted to a ceaseless curiosity by his situation. The critic's problem today is that too many works clamour for his notice: the rush of ideas and sensations must somehow be regulated. One way out of the difficulty is to retreat into specialized corners. The masses of secondary writings—detailed interpretations, biography, background studies—tend to fence off ever-narrowing fields; and the more that is known about each separate one the more hazardous it becomes to venture into several of these for the sake of a general view. In such a predicament the creative writers—poets and novelists who found their way naturally from one literature to another—allow the best chance of gaining a perspective. Every accomplished writer, when his works are spread out at the end, would seem to have realized in them a necessary pattern, the advance from one phase of experience to the next. If he is a witness whose authority can be felt, one in whom the age shows most fully alive, it is from his work that the critic may take his bearings. Too much of comparative study has gone into collocations that reveal little, or into the tracing of currents that never lose their brackishness. It should be animated by a sense of the imaginative world in which living writers move; by a recognition of their problems, of the reasons that impel them to seek out this or that contemporary or predecessor in some other part of the world's literature; and by an eagerness to retrace the steps of their original journey. Criticism, to use an old term, must be concreative. And this requires both agility and balance. It has to accompany the author into half-known areas and, while seeing with his eyes initially, to retain its own vision.

The ideal student of comparative literature—for it is to him we have been coming by way of the imaginative writers—will need time and patience; a conviction of where he is going; a keen eye for the local and particular; the awareness of historical context; an active belief that all literature is one and indivisible. Add to these temerity and reserve: he must not claim too much or enunciate too positively, yet be ready for risk.

The first problem awaiting him is that of national accent, which will be taken up in the next chapter.

2

National accent and tradition

In comparative study both the eye and the ear are important. The eye discerns what two or more literatures, two or more individual writers have in common. It fastens on themes, recurrent patterns, *topoi* in their development. It enables the reader to command a wide area, and to find categories. Northrop Frye is a critic who makes daring—indeed, extravagant—use of this faculty. But the ear must also be brought into play. To exercise it properly calls for a long and arduous training, because even in our own literature it may fail to respond with due subtlety. The ear catches the echoes of one writer in another; learns to distinguish the counterpoint of a work to its predecessor; recognizes the national accent; reveals the presence of an inner tradition. Erich Auerbach was unsurpassed in his cultivation of the ear. It allowed him to define the audience for which a work was written. He could show precisely the point at which originality breaks in, as when he discusses Dante's use of the idiom *da me stesso non vegno* (Auerbach, 1957, 159–60). By attending to tone and marking the movement of syntax, he could trace both continuity and change.

The reader who comes to a foreign writer (I speak of the Western family) should not have much difficulty in placing him within a general tradition. Here the eye serves with its clear categories. The writer appears as a symbolist poet or a novelist of manners. Once classified, however loosely—and it may often be loosely—he is accounted for, so far as the outer tradition goes. In the present chapter we must look for the inner tradition, the persistent and not always clearly definable quality that runs through a national literature and makes it unique.

There is a well-known essay by Eliot on Henry James, entitled 'The Hawthorne Aspect' (Dupee, 1947, 127-33). Following a hint or two from James himself, in his study of Hawthorne published in 1879, Eliot seeks to define the 'flavour' that denotes James 'positively a continuator of the New England genius'. With no writer established before him had James a relation so personal as with Hawthorne; but Eliot denies that this can be called influence on Hawthorne's side. Rather the two story-tellers are united in their sensibility and concerns, in their perception 'by antennae' of the mutual awareness between characters, and their very American sense of the past. Hawthorne was for James the most vivid presence in a whole group with whom he felt 'consciousness of kinship'. It included Emerson, Thoreau and Lowell, and was centred upon a small region of New England—'certain purlieus of Boston, with Concord, Salem, and Cambridge, Massachusetts'. Eliot does not use the word 'tone' to describe what distinguished that society—'a "something" there, a dignity, above the taint of commonness about some English contemporary, as, for instance, the more intelligent, better-educated, more alert Matthew Arnold'. But *tone* would do very well to express it. The quality is most clearly perceived in the voice of these writers.

That was how James saw the situation. Having said that 'a certain reflected light' in the pages of Hawthorne 'springs from' American life, he continues: 'the reader must look for his local and national quality between the lines of his writing and in the *indirect* testimony of his tone, his accent, his temper, of his very omissions and suppressions' (James, 1879, 124).* Many years later in *Notes of a Son and Brother* he associated the deaths, not widely spaced, of Hawthorne and Lincoln. It was then, as the Civil War reached a victorious end, that James felt a 'huge national emergence'; and probably the loss in these days of two Americans so unique disclosed to him, as nothing else had, his own feeling about America. Hawthorne died when James for the first time had acquired 'the full sweet sense of our one fine romancer's work' (James, 1956, 478). And it brought to him a recognition that seems to have cleared the way for his own talent. Hawthorne's work, he found,

was all charged with a *tone*, a full and rare tone of prose. . . . And the tone had been, in its beauty—for me at least— ever so appreciably American; which proved to what a use American matter could be put by an American hand: a consummation involving, it appeared, the happiest moral. For the moral was that an American could be an artist, one of the finest, without 'going outside' about it, as I liked to say; quite in fact as if Hawthorne had become one just by being American *enough*, by the felicity of how the artist in him missed nothing, suspected nothing, that the ambient air didn't affect him as containing (ibid., 480).

The writer who, as James did in 1864, grasps that he need not 'go outside' for his inspiration has achieved a rare and perhaps shortlived balance. He takes everything from 'the ambient air'—but there are few moments in history when the air of a particular place is so sheltered as to ring clear like that of Hawthorne's New England. In such moments we find a local culture that is complete

*James's italics, here and in the following quotations.

and sufficient. It allows a writer to treat the issues of the time and place in a serious manner. And because the community, however provincial, and however unsympathetic to the writer, does not lack sturdiness and self-reliance, the life that goes on there will sustain his art, even though frugally as with Hawthorne's.

Here the inner tradition will count for much. This appears above all in the case of Emily Dickinson, about whom Allen Tate has remarked: 'Miss Dickinson was a recluse; but her poetry is rich with a profound and varied experience' (Sewall, 1963, 19). He asks, 'Where did she get it?' and, ruling out the facile suggestions of some biographers which put everything down to unrequited love, he answers: it came from her situation. But that implies 'the whole complex of anterior fact, which was the social and religious structure of New England'. Living in Amherst, so near Northampton where rather more than a century earlier Jonathan Edwards had stirred Puritanism to a last blaze, Emily Dickinson could not mistake her heritage. The view of the world she would form must be controlled by it 'because I see—New Englandly'. Yet the language that carried her more than halfway to each discovery in the poems and letters knew no such limitation. She learned to express the local and relevant truth in the idioms that American experience had fashioned out of English. Behind her 'philology' musters the long and varied usage of English words, bringing with them a civilization ampler than her own. But the inflection she used was proudly American; her authority Webster's *American Dictionary* in the edition of 1847.

To see 'New Englandly' poses the need for a certain style, which Emily had to perfection. It requires that the tone should often be pitched deliberately low, in distrust of rhetoric; that the diction should be kept spare and precise; that irony should continually slip in and out of the discourse; and that the meaning should therefore carry a certain obliquity: 'Tell all the Truth but tell it slant.' Emily Dickinson's voice has to be heeded carefully. She is very direct in her feeling, yet more often than not she expresses it through indirection. So, like another New England poet, Robert Frost, she relies on our susceptibility to tone. Miss that and you have missed her meaning.

As with Frost, the meaning is uncomfortable. Emily Dickinson, in Allen Tate's words, 'attains to a mastery over experience by facing its utmost implications', which was also the way of her predecessor, Jonathan Edwards. She accepts the conflict between Nature, terrible yet exhilarating in its might, and the Puritan theology. The two irreconcilables are pitted against each other in her poetry. Hence the interplay there 'between abstraction and sensation'; and a very pronounced feeling for the duality in the English language which corresponds to the duality in her own thought. She uses, in a Shakespearian manner, 'the Latin for ideas and the Saxon for perception'. Emily Dickinson appears at the moment when Puritanism is losing its authority over American minds. But, as Tate has explained, the whole Puritan culture can still lend 'form and stability' to her own 'fresh perceptions of the world': 'it was an unconscious discipline timed to the pulse of her life'.

For Emily Dickinson there was no hindrance to writing as an American and to 'seeing New Englandly'. Her community held: she could say without forcing the sentiment that 'the Amherst Heart is plain and whole and permanent and warm'. The confidence of Amherst (as exemplified in her own authoritarian father) had not been shaken even by civil war. Its tenor of life ran steadily on, and to few, perhaps only to the dissident yet attached Emily, were the coming changes and upheavals visible. And where the community is unbroken, what Eliot said of tradition, that 'it cannot be inherited, and if you want it you must obtain it by great labour' (Eliot, 1960, 49), does not make sense. But the case is wholly different once the community has been exposed to a more powerful culture from outside. Hugh MacDiarmid, who wants to recover the native idiom in Scots verse, becomes 'a forlorn and isolated figure', to quote John Speirs (1962, 153). Even the last Scottish poet held to be truly national, Burns, lacked the fine European sense of Dunbar in the late Middle Ages. So when MacDiarmid gave out his slogan, 'Not Burns—Dunbar!' he was setting himself an impossible task. For too long the Scots language had been trampled on by men like Boswell, whose one desire was to speak a 'correct' English untainted by Scotticisms. With the language, as Speirs rightly says, 'a distinctive traditional life . . . has been destroyed'. It is vain to suppose that a living Scots poetic language can be gathered from out-of-the-way corners and old glossaries. The Scots poet has no option today but to write in English. However, there is the example of Yeats to encourage him. Speirs does not doubt that a national tone will come through if a writer 'possesses the honesty of genius' (ibid., 160). Any attempt at a willed 'Scottishness' offends that honesty. After all, Dunbar, than whom 'there was no more distinctively "Scottish" writer', did not make it 'his primary and deliberate aim to be so'. He was drawn to the 'European centre' (ibid., 54), and became national in his absorption with this larger concern.

Yeats has told of his problem, among other places, in the essay 'Poetry and Tradition' (1907). There he defines his own approach to the writing of a specifically Irish poetry in English. It should have 'a more subtle rhythm,

C

a more organic form' than had been achieved by his predecessors among the Irish. And it was 'always to re-member certain ardent ideas and high attitudes of mind which were the nation itself . . .' (Yeats, 1961, 248). Thus the Irish poet using English faced a twofold difficulty. The first part of it is expressed somewhat rhetorically by Stephen Dedalus in *A Portrait of the Artist as a Young Man*. He has been talking with an English priest. It caused him

a smart of dejection that the man to whom he was speaking was a countryman of Ben Jonson. He thought:

The language in which we are speaking is his before it is mine. How different are the words *home, Christ, ale, master,* on his lips and on mine! I cannot speak or write these words without unrest of spirit. His language, so fami-liar and so foreign, will always be for me an acquired speech. I have not made or accepted its words. My voice holds them at bay. My soul frets in the shadow of his language (Joyce, 1963, 189).

The Catholic and the Celt is complaining here, the native Irishman who has been excluded from his patrimony. Yeats, of Protestant and English stock, had his rights in the language and at some pains was able to find his tradition, that of 'Goldsmith and Burke, Swift and the Bishop of Cloyne' ('The Seven Sages'), who had lived in 'that one Irish century that escaped from darkness and confusion' (Yeats, 1964, 213). But always at the back of his mind there was a certain discomfort, even perhaps the 'unrest of spirit' that Dedalus felt, because he wanted to communicate with another Ireland. This Ireland entered Joyce's book in the form of 'Davin, the peasant student', who became a friend of Stephen's: 'His nurse had taught him Irish and shaped his rude imagination by the broken lights of Irish myth' (Joyce, 1963, 180).

The other aspect of the difficulty was one that made life complicated for Yeats almost from the beginning. Irish nationalism—intense, narrow and doctrinaire— blocked his path and distrusted the free imagination. It sought to circumscribe him at every turn, as it did a writer whom he was one of the first to recognize as truly national, John Synge: 'All the past had been turned into a melodrama with Ireland for blameless hero and poet. . . .' The Young Ireland movement 'had sought a nation unified by political doctrine alone, a subservient art and letters aiding and abetting' (Yeats, 1955, 204–6). The tradition it wanted to impose would be one-sided, unrealistic, and doomed to sterility.

Yeats knew what should replace it. Like the rest, he 'found [his] symbols of expression in Ireland', but did so 'while seeing all in the light of European literature' (Yeats, 1961, 248). He may have guided Synge to the Aran Islands and a vanishing peasant world, but his own imagination was English-bred, urban and complex. Gradually he found his way to the Anglo-Irish culture of Swift and Berkeley, which had flourished in their time as a tardy Renaissance coming to Ireland. Yeats may have been led to exaggerate, like the student in his play, *The Words upon the Window-pane*. But surely his instinct was right when it revealed to him the accent of Swift 'in O'Leary or in Taylor, or in the public speech of our statesmen . . . This instinct for what is near and yet hidden is in reality a return to the sources of our power, and therefore a claim made upon the future' (Yeats, 1964, 214). The Irishmen of the eighteenth century whom he admired had 'found in England the opposite that stung their own thought into expression and made it lucid' (Yeats, 1961, 402). Yeats brought an unforced Irish accent into his poetry, a poetry that could be true

> To cold Clare rock and Galway rock and thorn,
> To that stern colour and that delicate line
> That are our secret discipline . . .
>   ('In Memory of Major Robert Gregory'.)

And this he achieved by holding it against the model of English poetry, at the right distance. In 'The Municipal Gallery Revisited' he uses an image that had pleased him before—'No fox can foul the lair the badger swept'—and no doubt it pleased him for being drawn '. . . out of Spenser and the common tongue'. The last line points to the double ancestry of Yeats's diction.

By glancing at Hawthorne and Emily Dickinson, and at the dilemmas of MacDiarmid and Yeats, I hope to have shown the ways in which a national accent can be set on a language that has become supra-national. We have now to examine more closely the idea of tradition. A few indications have already been given in the preceding pages; but one of them needs to be taken a little farther. Tradition is manifested to the ear in a particular tone, not always recognizable to the foreigner. When a tone persists through many historical changes it is safe to infer that something like a spiritual identity has continued. To speak of 'national character' would be misleading, and indeed that fiction might well give way to another (without permitting any mystical overtones)—Lawrence's 'spirit of place'. The genius of a language will survive social change though not transplantation. Its native tone depends on the place where it is spoken, on the natural background no less than the human *milieu*. Pasternak has written of a scene that rhymes with a particular poet's work, the summer with Lermontov, geese and snow with Pushkin; and Stevens entitled one of his last poems 'A

Mythology should reflect Its Landscape'. It would seem
that the inner tradition needs a local base, and cannot
easily go back earlier than the acquisition of this. For
example, Shakespeare, the poet of an England just ceasing
to be medieval and Catholic, may not communicate with
the American today so directly as Walt Whitman from
nineteenth-century Long Island or Melville from nineteenth-century New York. We may recall that the
elegy Robert Lowell made for his cousin lost at sea, *The
Quaker Graveyard in Nantucket*, was modelled on
Lycidas. It had originally 194 lines for Milton's 193;
the metre and cadence are similar; certain lines carry the
ring of Milton's speech. A broad similarity of theme led
to this convergence. And yet Lowell's poem stands no
more than tangentially to Milton's. The real presences in
it belong to the New England terrain, Thoreau, from
whose *Cape Cod* it has taken the description of a wrecked
immigrant ship and a drowned girl, and Melville, who
sent the *Pequod* on her voyage after the White Whale
from Nantucket (Staples, 1962, 45–6, 101–3). An American
poet cannot ignore the stronger voices of his own tradition. Even T. S. Eliot, who once claimed that it was only
the American who could become a true European (Dupee,
1947, 124), reverts to 'the bent golden-rod and the lost sea
smell', to the New England thrush and the Mississippi;
and all these predilections give the clue to ingrained
American attitudes, an American genius.

'Spirit of place' is a reality for the poetic imagination,
and the traditional most clearly speaks through the local.
Anna Akhmatova in her fifties wrote a few lines of
tribute to a poet whom she still recognized as 'the
teacher', Innokenty Annensky. Not only temperament
and a common anguish united them, but also a particular
place: Tsarskoe Selo (now Pushkin), with its palaces,
statues and lime-trees. Here, as she recalled in one early

poem, 'A swarthy lad strayed down the alleys', Pushkin in his schooldays dropping there his three-cornered hat and the 'dog-eared volume of Parny'. All Akhmatova's poetical character, her delicacy and force and the self-command that enabled her to dominate suffering, seem to have been moulded by the tradition of Tsarskoe and Petersburg. Her special note harmonizes not only with Pushkin, but with his predecessor, Derzhavin, the court poet of Catherine's day; and through it can also be heard the true Dostoevskian timbre. For her, Leningrad at the end of the Second World War could momentarily

> seem an ancient lithograph
> Not first-class but perfectly decent
> Of, one would suppose, the seventies,

and the city brought back 'Dostoevsky's Russia'. As another St. Petersburg poet, Mandelstam, once remarked, she learned her psychological exactitude from the Russian novel, and particularly from Dostoevsky. The axis of her imaginative life ran through Tsarskoe and Petrograd, through Pushkin, Dostoevsky and Annensky. She had become inseparable from Leningrad and its classical authors:

> My shadow is on your walls,
> My reflection in the canals.

Lionel Trilling has said: '... it is not possible to conceive of a person standing beyond his culture. His culture has brought him into being in every respect except the physical, has given him his categories and habits of thought, his range of feeling, his idiom and tones of speech' (1966, xii). And this culture, as I have tried to show, cannot be separated from its environment. The writer achieves his balance, comes into full possession of his identity, when he has explored that culture to the depths and found there the sources to sustain him. Antonio Machado, regarded by many today as the foremost poet of Spain in modern times, found such a source in the fifteenth-century *Coplas* of Jorge Manrique:

> *Nuestras vidas son los ríos*
> *que van a dar a la mar,*
> *que es el morir ...*

These lines on the inexorable flow of life towards death, which he glossed in a short lyric stating

> Among my poets
> Manrique has an altar,

gave to his own poetry its ground-bass. Luis Cernuda could discern the rhythms of Manrique in Machado's 'rural meditations', 'Poem of a Day'; and emphasized that he was for Machado 'the Spanish poet to be admired most'. This rapport with Manrique depends on a special feeling for the Castilian tongue and an acceptance of the Castilian landscape, which had for Machado certain qualities not alien to 'The First Book of Moses, called Genesis'. Castilian was 'the imperial language' of his country; he honoured 'Castile that made Spain'. Yet Machado, like so many Spanish poets of this age, was no Castilian himself, but an Andalusian. The best of his poetry, as Cernuda insists, came from his being the latter, and Juan Ramón Jiménez saw him as 'the delicate disciple of Bécquer', also an Andalusian poet. Machado loved in Bécquer's work the purity and lightness of form, and the way it moved 'on the margin of logic', a 'genuine poetry' with its own perceptible dialectic. And he was fully aware that the Andalusian tone and feeling differed from the

Castilian. His review of the Malagan poet Moreno Villa defines the Andalusian element as revealed in a 'balance ... between the intuitive and the conceptual', 'between the poet's feeling and the cold outline of things'. Here then is the prime sensibility, Machado's own as that of the poet he describes. For him, the addition of Castile made it responsive to the whole Spanish heritage.

In all these examples one fact will have been noted: the writer's filial relation to language. The quality of his thought and feeling is apportioned to him by his mother tongue. He may extend here and there its possibilities; but once a language has been realized in literature, once the 'Shakespearian moment' has occurred, thought and feeling are controlled in a thousand specific ways. Pasternak—the passage is often quoted—tells how there comes in the process of writing poetry a sudden reversal of forces (Pasternak, 1958, 391). The language itself takes over from the poet, shaping his thoughts and utterance; and he begins to feel himself the initiator of something that pursues its own purposes. The state of inspiration means perhaps more than anything else being possessed by a language. The poet achieves an extraordinary freedom and boldness of expression, as though the language has begun to create of its own accord, 'an eagle mewing her mighty youth'. In such moments there is a renovation of old insights committed to the language, a rehabilitation of the memory that exists in words. When the language uses a poet like this, he transcends his own powers; but he does not transcend the powers inherent in the language.

It may be said that, while the languages of the world today are continually learning from each other and meeting in common experience, they also insist jealously on their uniqueness. The mother tongue may admit stepchildren, an occasional Joseph Conrad; but it is to be guarded as peculiar to ourselves, and in certain ways incommunicable. It has the duty of maintaining our selfhood, our traditional emphases and reserves; the privacy of the individual is bound up with the intimacy of language. No foreigner can ever penetrate all the recesses of a language, but he may learn to recognize its characteristic modes and to catch its intonation. The student of comparative literature has to accept that here is a threshold on which he must halt. Half the fascination in his work will derive from a growing sense of the irreducibly singular, the idiosyncratic, that gives every literature its own beauty and its own enigma.

3

The mind of Europe

No single literature stands complete. This is particularly true of Europe and its offshoot the Americas. Behind any one literature an ampler tradition becomes visible: it is seen to participate in a culture with shared assumptions —even if these are now wearing thin. Europe has generally known internal discord, and yet through the centuries it has contrived to keep a civilization that is essentially one from the Atlantic to the Urals. There are obviously differences, and quite significant ones, between the Western and the Eastern forms of that civilization, as they have developed since the Roman Empire and the Christian Church fell into two parts. All the same, few would quarrel with such terms as 'the mind of Europe' (Eliot) or *la conscience européenne* (Paul Hazard), though these put their emphasis mainly on Western Europe. A real community of thought and feeling, despite all the contradictions, has existed. From the time of Cicero until perhaps the last hundred years literature prescribed the forms of conduct for Christian and humanist alike. The dignity of literature was cherished by such men as Ben Jonson and Samuel Johnson: they felt that society owed to the scholar and man of letters, hardly less than to the divine, a conception of its true self. Matthew Arnold could speak with the same conviction, though already in his time literature was losing its hold.

A common ideal to be truly effective must rely on a large body of ideas and attitudes which are not disputed. When Arnold was treating of urbanity, of the centrally placed intelligence, of criticism as a great civilizing agency and as a corrective to loose thinking and headstrong selfishness, he assumed that education meant humane letters. This was not the view of T. H. Huxley and of many people living in the 'intensely modern world of the United States'. Arnold, however, insisted that if a choice had to be made between humane letters and natural science, those who were not gifted with 'exceptional and overpowering aptitudes for the study of nature' should keep to the older discipline: 'Letters will call out their being at more points, will make them live more' (Arnold, 1889, 129). We can now see that Arnold was appealing to an authority which had only a few decades to run before it collapsed altogether. The confidence in humane letters which he voiced so bravely had behind it long centuries of education in the Greek and Roman classics and the Hebrew scriptures. This more than anything made it possible for him to proclaim as his ideal 'a criticism which regards Europe as being, for intellectual and spiritual purposes, one great confederation, bound to a joint action and working to a common result; and whose members have, for their proper outfit, a knowledge of Greek, Roman, and Eastern antiquity, and of one another' (Arnold, 1865, 39). That this confederation was not limited to Western Europe becomes plain from his preliminary remarks in the essay on Tolstoy:

The famous English novelists have passed away, and have left no successors of like fame. It is not the English novel,

therefore, which has inherited the vogue lost by the French
novel. It is the novel of a country new to literature, or at
any rate unregarded, till lately, by the general public of
readers: it is the novel of Russia. The Russian novel has
now the vogue, and deserves to have it. If fresh literary
productions maintain this vogue and enhance it, we shall
all be learning Russian (Arnold, 1888, 254).

But when he extended his view to take in the literature
of an unknown language, Arnold kept to the standards
elaborated by classical scholars, humanists, and believers
in the European tradition.

Today that tradition has weakened perceptibly. Few of
us know the Bible with even half the thoroughness of our
great-grandfathers, who heard it regularly in church or
chapel and at family prayers. Fewer still know the
classics, or read them with any enjoyment except in
translation. Classical studies have dwindled to become
one branch of learning among many, and even a somewhat drooping branch; while the study of literature
(which in Arnold's day presupposed a classical core) has
lost ground steadily, and seems to many people less important than history, political science, sociology or psychology. The so-called 'crisis in the humanities' comes
to a head in the plight of classical studies. Their diminish-
ing has prompted a defence of English as the final bastion,
the base from which a criticism such as Arnold desired
can sally forth and reconquer the field. I return to this
topic in Chapter 5.

You cannot go far in comparative study without feeling the need to bring back the lost dimension. What gave
Arnold his authority as a critic, endowing him with a
large and uninterrupted perspective, was his familiarity
with the European past—to speak more accurately, with
the Mediterranean past. Hebrew religion, Greek myth

and philosophy, Latin decorum—all these imparted a texture to the mind. They furnished it, and they brought an ultimate confidence and a serenity which we cannot hope for today. A century before Arnold, these qualities are manifested in Johnson, whose grasp of antiquity made him heir to the full tradition. It might be contended that Johnson was a national bigot, that his warm humanity did not save him from narrow prejudices, that he was too much what Arnold calls Carlyle, 'a genuine son of Great Britain', with abundant 'self-will and eccentricity'. Merely to glance at Carlyle and then back at Johnson will show how little the charge sticks. Johnson came up to Oxford, as we learn from Boswell, with a wide and miscellaneous reading. He knew Latin literature in and out, 'though but little Greek'. One of Johnson's first undertakings at Oxford was to make a translation, much esteemed, into Latin verse of Pope's *Messiah*, 'as a Christmas exercise'. He wrote Latin poems all through his life, sometimes to express feeling which would have looked raw and naked in English. By setting personal anxieties or fears in the frame of classical reference he could acknowledge and control them. Several of his more intimate poems adopt the measure and tone of early Christian hymns. He could draw on the Roman liturgy as on the classics. In the same way Latin prose seemed to him more fitting than the vernacular for a memorial tablet. He refused to give up his Latin epitaph on Goldsmith because 'he would never consent to disgrace the walls of Westminster Abbey with an English inscription'.

The world in which Johnson and Gibbon grew up had not lost its sense of continuity with the world of Cicero or Marcus Aurelius. A new Augustan age looked with complacency at its predecessor in Rome. The Ancients and Moderns belonged, in spite of the quarrel, to one civilization. Already a new conception of history which would dwell on the uniqueness of each phase in human development, on the otherness of the past, was beginning to play tricks with the old clarity of vision. But for Johnson all human history had the same features, and what had been true in Rome must be no less true in the Strand or in China. History was composed of personal dramas that involved right or wrong moral choice. Later on, the Italian *Risorgimento* would still form its ideals by that mirror for revolutionaries until 1848, Plutarch's *Lives*. History in its finer moments was something to emulate. The French Revolution and Empire saw themselves as the heirs of Rome.

Johnson and his contemporaries turned habitually to this grand example. The Roman background 'lies behind Pope's work, and much of Swift's and Fielding's, like a charged magnetic field, a reservoir of attitudes whose energy can be released into their own creations at a touch' (Maynard Mack in Clifford, 1959, 34). And this notion of excellence, which embraced 'a mighty and civilized tradition in arts, morals, government', enabled a writer to judge his own epoch by the past. The schoolboy, almost without realizing it, acquired the habit of comparative study. If he knew Greek, which was less common, he must continually notice the contrast between Homer and Virgil, Demosthenes and Cicero, Thucydides and the Roman historians. The same kind of comparison was forced on him daily as he read Virgil and Milton, Pope and Horace. The classics may have been written in a dead language—dead, that is to say, on the streets and in working life. As a written language it had not died, and in the form of quotation it often came to the lips of the educated. Once, however, their descendants gave up pronouncing Latin in the old way as though the words were English, the classics became foreign. The new historical consciousness demanded this should be so. But the change signified, without being the sole cause, the closing of a frontier.

A poet like Dryden or Pope could count on the 'common reader' to supply a background of biblical and classical reference. Few writings on current affairs were taken up more eagerly by the public than *Absalom and Achitophel* in 1681. The poem attacked Shaftesbury and the Whigs for their support of Monmouth as heir to the throne in place of the Catholic James Duke of York. But it assumed that the parallel with a story in the Second Book of Samuel would not be lost on the general reader. And a further patterning was imposed by references to the temptation scene in *Paradise Lost*. Thus a trenchant political satire brought into play echoes of the Old Testament, of the modern English epic, and of its classical forebears. Half the pleasure in Augustan poetry, and in Renaissance poetry too, derives from the awareness of a Latin original which must be present to the mind. Certain writings, such as Pope's *Imitations of Horace*, challenged a direct comparison. Others, like the epistle Dryden wrote to his 'honoured kinsman, John Driden, of Chesterton', can not fully be appreciated without a fair knowledge of the Latin poetry that celebrates rural retirement, though the imitation here is much freer: it matches tone and attitude rather than whole passages of a general design. And sometimes the full resonance of a poem will depend on our not missing an allusion. In his elegy 'To the Memory of Mr Oldham', a plain and reserved tribute to the younger satirist, Dryden pulls out two stops that give a subtle vibrato. Both are references to the *Aeneid*. In the first he recalls the friendship of Nisus and Euryalus (v.294–361; ix.176–449); in the second those lines on the death of Marcellus her nephew at which the Empress is said to have fainted when Virgil first spoke them (vi.854–86). By thus alluding to two famous and pathetic episodes in a poem that most of his readers knew almost by heart, Dryden imparted a depth to his elegy that is now concealed.

Virgil was particularly honoured in the Middle Ages for the fortuitous reason that his fourth *Eclogue* appeared to announce the birth of Christ. Even if this interpretation could not have been made, his prestige as the poet of Rome and of its imperial destiny would have proved almost irresistible. Dante represented himself in the *Divine Comedy* as the favoured son of this poet, and indeed it was Virgil who found for him a style, a tone, a final dimension (Auerbach, 1957, 173). The *Divine Comedy* legitimizes Virgil the great precursor in Christian legend. It also demonstrates more clearly than any other work that the Christian era still drew much of its intellectual energy, and fostered its imagination, from classical sources. Dante did not appropriate Virgil; it might be truer to say that Virgil appropriated him, that a tenacious and deep-set tradition had once more prevailed. Virgil does not please all critics today, any more than Milton does: his voice may, like Milton's, sound over-magniloquent for our time; yet this effect was natural to him, a gift of the Latin tongue. Virgil could not be so accessible to Milton, at such a remove in time and place, as earlier he had been to Dante. The effort of assimilating his manner led Milton to overburden English with Latin words and constructions. For an Italian poet, whose vernacular touched Virgil's Latin at every turn, the difficulties facing Milton hardly existed. To understand Virgil was to communicate with his own world.

We may recall Eliot's claim that England too should be reckoned a 'Latin' country (Curtius, 1953, 35). Some of the virtues peculiar to Latin were annexed by English when it came into its own. Shakespeare is a master of Latinate grandeur when he has need of it; the Authorized

Version puts on Latin and relinquishes it much in the manner of a priest changing his vestments during the service. Owen Barfield has shown how a Latin word like *ruin* acquired even fuller life when it entered our language, thanks chiefly to Shakespeare (Barfield, 1952, 113–26). There is free commerce between the Latin and English languages, though a certain control has to be exercised over imports. A 'Latin' country in the true sense England could never become, since the native English element of our speech holds the Latin in check, and throws off the borrowed panoply when it has need of the simplest and most moving effects. But no language of Europe outside the Romance family, and hence no literature, stands in a closer relation with the Latin heritage. And it is the qualities making up that heritage which have laid the European tradition. This became a more various and splendid thing than its Latin nucleus. But through Latin Greece was mediated to the other peoples of Western Europe; and for centuries the Hebrew Bible addressed them through the Latin Vulgate.

Perhaps the master quality in classical writing, that to which all the others contribute, is a natural sense of scale. Forster's expatriate Englishman recognises this on his return to Europe: 'The buildings of Venice, like the mountains of Crete and the fields of Egypt, stood in the right place, whereas in poor India everything was placed wrong. He had forgotten the beauty of form....' What Venice had to offer him was 'something more precious than mosaics and marbles...: the harmony between the works of man and the earth that upholds them, the civilization that has escaped muddle, the spirit in a reasonable form, with flesh and blood subsisting'. And he concludes that 'The Mediterranean is the human norm' (Forster, 1924, 283).

Forster's predilection for Italy may seem to lend addi-

D

tional proof that he belongs to 'the fag-end of Victorian liberalism'. There is a romantic strain to be discerned here; and it may be that anyone from these islands must fail to see the Mediterranean ideal so dispassionately, even so prosaically, as those who have lived with it always. But Forster has seized on the essential point, that this formal beauty rests on an intimate alliance between man and Nature, and is made up of 'works and days', the labour of man performed in the fields according to the farmer's calendar. The *Georgics* no less than the *Aeneid* have determined the classical mode of feeling which never permits values to be confounded or buildings to be 'placed wrong'. Man is still agrarian man; he accepts the discipline of the soil, the fidelities of a fixed home, a traditional and undeviating order. This has been the foundation for European poetry, and its accepted norm, where-ever the classical note has made itself heard—principally, of course, in the Latin countries, but with constant renewals in almost every corner of Europe. The harmony that Forster has called Mediterranean still dominates the mind of Europe, even today when poetry can do little more than mark its overthrow by modern conditions of life. Antonio Machado has said that it was Rousseau who first outmoded 'the rustic, the essentially Georgic, feeling for earth which is worked', a feeling that he derives from Virgil and finds undiminished in Lope de Vega. City life had surfeited Rousseau, but between the small Mediterranean city and the fields surrounding it there was no quarrel. Indeed, urbanity is one element in the Georgic tone.

'Natural piety'—to use Wordsworth's phrase—enters largely into it. Virgil had been the poet of the *di agrestes*, the old rural gods (Bailey, 1935, 34); and it was Virgil who presented under so many aspects the notion of *pietas* in his *Aeneid*. This attitude implies a right relation

with the gods, the family, and the State (ibid., 80): the
man who practises *pietas* thereby demonstrates that he
has acquired the measure of all things. Scale therefore
depends on a moral consciousness (which is exactly what
Pope says in his *Epistle to Burlington*: without 'sense'
there can be neither good building nor disinterested
action.) Much of European poetry has endeavoured to
call back the *pietas* of earlier times when faith and
morals were supposed to be simpler: Horace warns the
Roman of his day that the temples must be restored, the
images cleansed of their grime; nothing can save Rome
but the old discipline bred by poverty on the farmstead
(*Odes*, iii.6). Dante assigns to his ancestor Cacciaguida
the same testimony: Florence within her ancient walls
had been orderly, sensible and upright: '*si stava in pace,
sobria e pudica*' (*Paradiso*, xv, 97–9). Wordsworth in all
seriousness can commend the effects of

> breathing in content
> The keen, the wholesome, air of poverty,
> And drinking from the well of homely life
> (*Excursion*, i.305-7.)

Among modern poets none, I think, had so developed a
sense of piety as Wordsworth. In the same poem of
Margaret and her ruined cottage from which I have just
quoted the Wanderer stood by her disused spring

> And eyed its waters till we seemed to feel
> One sadness, they and I. For them a bond
> Of brotherhood is broken : time has been
> When, every day, the touch of human hand
> Dislodged the natural sleep that binds them up
> In mortal stillness; and they ministered
> To human comfort   (485-91.)

And elsewhere he has written a line which sums up in one memorable image the essence of piety: 'We talk about the dead by our fire-sides' ('The Brothers', 179). Pound's denunciation of *usura*, 'sin against nature', invokes once again the old simplicities without which life loses its wholesomeness and is palsied (*Cantos* xlv). For 2,000 years this note has been constant in European poetry.

With piety there belongs an acceptance of human nature—to be found in Horace and Montaigne—acknowledging its needs, and not disguising such weaknesses as cowardice, self-indulgence, or vanity. (The Prince in Lampedusa's novel, *Il gattopardo*, reveals himself unashamedly as he is; and one may compare his attitude with that of James's Italian Prince in *The Golden Bowl*, whose moral sense was more like a 'tortuous stone staircase—half-ruined into the bargain' than the 'lightning elevator' of the Americans.) Horace may be distasteful to the twentieth century. His compromise and mediocrity do not appeal in the age following Dostoevsky and Melville. But the Horatian pattern, the Horatian tone, have continually been adopted, and not only in the Mediterranean countries. Pope and Thackeray (the latter being at the same time an uneasy Victorian) took up his stance. However, the bland self-sufficiency of Horace, the resignation and irony, the wariness and elegance and the prosaic common sense, are qualities that seem indigenous to the Mediterranean scene. We can accept from Horace what we find almost intolerable in Yeats:

> I am content to follow to its source
> Every event in action or in thought;
> Measure the lot; forgive myself the lot!
> ('A Dialogue of Self and Soul'.)

The last feature on which I want to dwell is decorum.
This necessitates a rhetoric not always acceptable to our
ears. Johnson used it most effectively when he wrote
about Garrick: 'I am disappointed by that stroke of death,
which has eclipsed the gaiety of nations. . . .' The nations
at most were the few inhabiting the British Isles, and
there is a noble exaggeration about the tribute. Johnson,
it will be noted, gains his effect by choosing words of
Latin and Romance origin—*disappointed, eclipsed, gaiety,
nations*—though the plain cause of his sorrow is given
in the simplest and most immediate English words—'that
stroke of death'. By 'decorum' we mean just this controlled exaggeration, in which restraint and hyperbole
meet. It would require no great search to produce many
examples from Latin poetry, and from the poetry of
Italy, France and Spain. At its best the rhetoric is
governed by a strong sense of the actual, and an under-
lying sobriety. When Horace is overcome by grief for
his friend Quintilius, he feels that restraint is
unthinkable—

> *Quis desiderio sit pudor aut modus*
> *Tam cari capitis?*
>
> (*Odes*, i.24.)

Yet in the moment of abandon he still remembers *pudor*
and *modus*, propriety and measure. An instinct for propriety was behind Verlaine's celebrated comment on *In
Memoriam*: 'when he should have been broken-
hearted, he had many reminiscences' (Yeats, 1955, 342).
Compare the poems of bereavement written by Machado
and by Hardy in the same year, 1913. Machado, aided
by that Castilian reticence which he had come to prize—

> *como el olivar,*
> *mucho fruto lleva,*
> *poca sombra da—*

writes half a dozen grave and perfectly modulated lyrics full of anguish for his dead wife, though sometimes allusion is made to her only in the last line. Hardy felt, as we know, the keenest remorse when his wife died; he may well have been broken-hearted; but there are innumerable reminiscences of her in his poetry during the sixteen years he survived. The theme grows obsessive, after its first memorable statements, whereas decorum has saved Machado's pain for the briefest and finest utterance. This decorum, if it derives from the Mediterranean world, bears the imprint of its own landscape, where detail is clear, and even bold, but never becomes rudely salient. The uniform light keeps everything in its place; and values are controlled.

As a final instance of these Latin virtues in style and feeling, we may consider one of the most celebrated poems written in this century, Paul Valéry's *Le Cimetière marin*. It is a work penetrated with the Mediterranean light: *midi le juste*, the noonday as accurate and impartial arbiter, brings all to a severe perfection:

> *La vie est vaste, étant ivre d'absence,*
> *Et l'amertume est douce, et l'esprit clair.*

The poem could be called a distillation of Latin feelings and attitudes (written by the man who was afterwards to believe that Europe had come to an end). Both setting and theme are deeply traditional. The graveyard— *'Composé d'or, de pierre et d'arbres sombres'*—makes a plea for human dignity and purpose when all around is an alien and timeless sea, and nothing personal remains of the dead. Inexorably the poem states that human life, troubling the immense and unregarding serenity, must yield very soon to annihilation: *'Tout va sous terre et rentre dans le jeu!'* Yet the act of contemplation satisfies and rallies the will to face life anew: *'Le vent se lève!... Il faut tenter de vivre!'* Valéry may now seem the last classical poet of France. *Le Cimetière marin* is in its way a definitive poem: it speaks for a whole civilization that may not return. But so long as Europe remains a confederation of thought and feeling, the Latin note will not be missing from it.

4

Notes on translation

Something has been said earlier about the intimacy of a language. I remarked at the close of Chapter 2 that the student, however perceptive, will meet eventually in foreign literature a threshold at which he must halt. Machado has assigned to his imaginary poet and pedagogue Mairena the view that no more than a single language—the one we live and think in—can be fully alive for us. We must content ourselves with a merely formal and literary knowledge of any others. Translation hopes to ignore the threshold, and to make itself an inmate of the foreign culture—but the hope is delusive. Whenever a language has been used to express the truths of imagination, whether in poetry or prose, the resulting work will be rooted all the more firmly in the untranslatable. Words charged with meaning cannot be replaced; the connotations they hold are too tenuous, and further meaning is as it were hidden between them—in the play of counterpoint, the dramatizing movement, the emphasis that comes from slight irregularities of position. And also the native ear can detect tones which may be imparted by a single word. Dante in the fifth canto of the *Paradiso* writes on the significance of a vow:

> *Quest' ultima già mai non vi cancella,*
>   *se non servata*   (46–7.)

—it can be cancelled only by being kept—and, as Cosmo observed, the Latinity of the word *servata* aims to give livelier expression to the Roman quality of the thought. Again A. S. Orlov has shown how the word *sushchiy* (present participle of the verb *to be* in Russian) acquires a different tonality in two examples from Pushkin. In the first, from *Boris Godunov*, the abbot agrees that the pretender's claim is heresy, and he repeats the phrase *sushchaya eres'*. Here the word has an archaic and ecclesiastical ring, as if he should say: 'veritable heresy'. In the second, Pushkin's verses on his 'monument' declare that 'every tongue existing therein [throughout Russia] will name me' and here the effect of *suschiy* is magnificent and solemn.

A work translated can never be more than an oil painting reproduced in black and white. The texture has changed. Of course the broad arrangement of masses and planes will be no less clear, and perhaps even quite delicate nuances are not lost. However, the primal harmony has given place to something less finely calculated. Whenever the imagination is working at its full capacity —whether in a lyric, a play, or a novel—it organizes the material with a degree of subtlety and comprehensiveness that no translation could ever match. The unity of the completed work draws together a multitude of converging details. It is bound to be impoverished in translation, though to what extent will depend on the form, whether prose or verse, and if verse whether short and lyrical, or narrative and sustained.

Even the most scrupulous rendering of a foreign work will tend to distortion. Arnold warned the translator against a 'mist of alien modes of thinking, speaking and feeling' which stands between him and the original (Arnold, 1960, 103). However clearly he may have seen the original, a translator must yield to the pressures of his own language. They will take over the business, with or without his consent. This can be seen glaringly in Gide's versions of *Hamlet* and of *Antony and Cleopatra*. He understood perfectly well the risks of translating Shakespeare, the disfigurement that might follow; and yet with all his intelligence—not hampered by a verse form, but apparently finding even French prose intractable—he altered Shakespeare tone for tone, and spirit for spirit. Here the well-known incompatibilities of the French genius and the English aided his downfall; but every translator, perfect though his sympathies may be with the original, subtly and involuntarily displaces it so that it may be realigned in the order of his own literature.

We must know the limits of our perception here. The English reader is often shocked, for example, at the lack of discrimination (so it seems to him) shown by the foreigner who exalts Byron and Wilde above all our nineteenth-century authors, or who turns lightly from Keats to Swinburne. The mistakes are gross enough, to be explained by the fact that Byron and Wilde (in Ortega's phrase) have less to leave behind at the Customs, and that Swinburne has possibly more in common with Hugo than with Keats. Eliot may be right in asserting that good poetry is recognizable even to those unskilled in the actual language, that it 'can communicate before it is understood' (Eliot, 1965, 8). This faculty of divining what is poetry and what isn't depends not at all on philology, though I suppose philology will nurture it. We must regard it as an unusual gift, and chiefly one made to the poets; nor do they have it always at their command. The reader who learns to judge poetry as most of us learn, by a painful self-education in which the moments of insight are few and far between, will not form any illusions about his response to foreign poetry. He cannot hope that in more than one or two languages will he attain the quickness of feeling to comprehend why a thing is said in a particular way, or what constitutes poetic daring. The more intimately he knows his own language, the nearer he will come to appreciating the felicities of expression in a foreign writer. There can be a happy instinct that brings help in these matters; those who have literary sense, which like every other sense is improved by practice, will soon get familiar with the contours of a language, its usual forms and tendencies; and so let themselves be guided by it, like one learning a new dance. However, we should not presume, even from the closest acquaintance, that all the vibrations of a phrase are registered on our ear.

Poetry requires the closest attention, and the most humility in a foreign reader. But the case is not wholly different with novels. Narrative, both in verse and prose, can be followed step for step through a good translation. It loses little of its structure and little therefore of the essential meaning—if the general pace and proportions are kept. Thousands of readers without Russian have responded to *Anna Karenina* or *Crime and Punishment*. They are often moved by them more deeply than by most novels in their own language. One hesitates to suggest that a reading without benefit of Russian will be an imperfect reading. Yet the novel in translation has, to some degree, been isolated from where it belongs, within a particular phase of Russian culture. A whole fund of allusion is dissipated. Voices become thinner and less characteristic. And all the discriminations in the author's vocabulary, his peculiar tricks of emphasis and his pervading manner will hardly come through. From the story of *Anna Karenina* we are bound to infer Tolstoy's earnestness, but translation conceals the deliberate inelegance of his style, when he tried to set down impressions as they occur. The impetuosity and strained awareness of

Dostoevsky leap out of any page, even in translation; not so his peculiar Russian slyness, the mocking and slippery intelligence of his narrator's voice. Again, how could any translation do justice to all that is most English in Jane Austen—her numberless reserves and decencies, the coolness of her appraisals, the candid and equable light in which she lives, her precision of utterance, which is no less social than intellectual, resting on a whole series of exclusions? A novel that is conceived imaginatively will use language its own way and emerge the poorer in translation. The difficulties are plain where—as with Trimalchio in the novel by Petronius, or in the stories of Zoshchenko—the narrator's tone sets the angle at which we should approach the story. Missing the sound of his voice, as it unconsciously gives away all that he is, the reader loses a certain finesse in the implied criticism. And this would seem to be true of every good novel, where, however discreetly, by perhaps no more than the placing of an adverb or the ironic repetition of an abstract noun, the author reveals that he too is watching.

Comparative study will be at its best when the critic, like Edmund Wilson, moves easily from one language to another. But few people have the faculty (and it may in the wrong hands even prove dangerous). I doubt whether much can be achieved in this study without Arnold's condition that 'every critic should try and possess one great literature, at least, besides his own; and the more unlike his own, the better' (Arnold, 1865, 39). With two or three literatures open to him, and it is essential that his own should be among these, the critic may hope to discern the general pattern, and to find out various relationships. But to complete the inquiry he will almost for certain have to depend at some point on translations. These can help him at the periphery; they allow tentative conclusions to be drawn; sometimes they will accentuate one element or possibly the whole character of the main work he is considering. Europe alone has so many literatures, none of them negligible, that translation must be called in.

What are we entitled to demand from the translator? What bounds of possibility limit his art?

The first law of translation is clear: nothing can be taken as final. Every age views literature through the prism of its own preoccupations. These alter in line with the changes in human history. And it is the nature of a classic to present new facets in a new situation. This alone will explain the backwash of critical writing that any considerable work leaves behind in its progress through time. A translation, however impressive, cannot truly co-extend with the original. They are not, obviously, one and the same; the degrees of emphasis will be different; the translation belongs to a different stream in the world's literature, and the meeting of two streams is bound to result in cross-currents, unseen eddies, a hidden bias. The modern reader cannot doubt that the Schlegel-Tieck version of Shakespeare, for all its high merit, belongs to the age of Goethe. It has falsified Shakespeare, quite unconsciously, so that he becomes an honorary citizen of Weimar, with an unfamiliar discretion, a more even tone, and greater explicitness. It might be called a superb adaptation of Shakespeare to the German understanding at a particular time. But the German critic who writes on Shakespeare will have to banish the image created by Schlegel-Tieck, if he is looking for the authentic Shakespeare. So with the English Bible. Magnificent and irreplaceable, the Authorized Version is stamped all over with the characteristics of a particular epoch in the Anglican Church. The *New English Bible* aimed to strike away every association of the Scriptures with that epoch, and to give back the novelty,

the urgent colloquial freshness that the Koine Greek of
the New Testament originally had. Most critics have dis-
liked the slipshod and broken-down style of the *N.E.B.*;
but how far is the Authorized Version to be trusted?
It has been established for centuries now as the English
Bible, interpenetrating our national life and supplying a
thousand time-hallowed formulations. The careful reader
must bear in mind that he deals only with the *English*
Bible, and has no warrant to speak of the New Testament
in Greek or in Jerome's Latin.

A translation may have extraordinary claims to survive.
Pound has called the version of Ovid's *Metamorphoses*
by Golding 'the most beautiful book in the language';
Johnson thought Pope's *Iliad* 'the noblest version of poetry
which the world has ever seen'. Neither is much read
nowadays. Yet it is to translations of this order that
one would send those who cannot read the originals.
Golding remains an Elizabethan, Pope an Augustan, but
they were what few translators are—genuine poets. It is
always possible to discern their excesses or shortcomings
from an accurate prose version by some modern authority. They impart that sense of discovery which a
poet's translation shares with its original. A good version
ought to infect, even if the strain has been modified.
And the likelihood is that a poet will achieve one major
triumph, whatever incidental faults he may commit out
of deference to his own age. He should grasp that by
which a poem, narrative or dramatic or lyric, most
clearly attests to its being alive—the sustaining movement. Pope's Homer departs from the original in a
hundred ways: he would have done far better with Ovid,
one may often feel; and yet Arnold has to concede that
Pope brought his own rapidity to match Homer's. They
are different kinds of rapidity; but Pope in Arnold's view
has come nearer than the 'conscientiously literal' Cowper

who, by slowing down his *Iliad* to the pace of *Paradise Lost*, has spoiled everything. Arnold insists that 'the peculiar effect of a poet resides in his manner and movement, not in his words taken separately' (Arnold, 1960, 105). Pope has sinned against the manner of Homer in making it more refined; but a sin against movement is not only more serious, it is mortal.

The same difficulty arises in translating the novel. Proust was fortunate to have Scott Moncrieff as his translator (even though he botched the title of *A la recherche du temps perdu* by rendering it *Remembrance of Things Past*). Moncrieff embodied in his version the intricate, slowly uncoiling rhythms of Proust, which reveal the mind attentive to every least hint as it gathers up the evidence for a complex statement about perceiving. A translator of Flaubert has to listen acutely. There are obvious sound-effects in his description of things apprehended by sense. But he is also very particular about the fall of his clauses when dealing with the moral world:

> *Elle eut envie de se mettre dans les demoiselles
> de la Vierge. Mme Aubain l'en dissuada.*
> *Un événement considérable surgit: le mariage de Paul.*
> *(Un Cœur simple.)*

Elaborate rhythms are not much appreciated in our time. The translator wants to break them up, to escape from the world of Clarendon and Saint-Simon to that of Kipling and Hemingway. But good imaginative prose cannot dispense with the effects of rhythm organized through the paragraph (as indeed noticeably it is organized by Hemingway too). Destroy the rhythm, and the author's presence has been taken out.

We should ask of a translation that it regard the movement and therefore the density in its original. *Doctor Zhivago*, for instance, though very readable in the version of Max Hayward and Manya Harari, has to some extent quickened its pace, the translators now and again smoothing over the detail of Pasternak's more involved sentences. Thereby it has shed not a little density. The experience is here and there simplified; a few of the more tenuous connections drop out. So far as possible, the translator should hold impressions to their original order, even if this requires him to make an unusual demand upon English syntax. Too many verse translators feel a superstitious dread of altering the metrical form. They do not realize that a more serious infidelity may result. Every poem enacts an experience along a particular curve of impression and feeling, and so articulated that one detail precedes another. This dictates the essential rhythm, expressed in a particular metrical pattern. But the same pattern in a different language may easily frustrate that rhythm. The first duty of a translator must be to trace the necessary movement in a poem, the inner determinant of its shape, and not to part with that.

Translation is at its happiest when showing a true affinity with the original, a like-mindedness or even a personal bond. Here it encroaches upon imitation, the design of which allows the poet of a different time or country to adapt the original so that it serves for a new occasion. Pope was attracted to Horace or Johnson to Juvenal because each felt that the Roman poet had put very well what needed saying once more. They discerned a resemblance between the ancient and modern worlds, they found in Horace or Juvenal an attitude which appealed to them—though Pope has more in common with Horace than Johnson with Juvenal—and were thus able to play a descant upon the original work. Their kind of imitation assumes that the reader will keep the earlier poem in view when he judges its modern counterpart. He is not to miss the ironic contrast in Pope's *Epistle to Augustus* between the patron of Horace and the philistine George II:

> Oh! could I mount on the Maeonian wing.
> Your Arms, your Actions, your repose to sing!
> ... But Verse, alas! your Majesty disdains,
> And I'm not us'd to Panegyric strains ...
>
> (ll.394–5, 404–5.)

Not all imitations rely to this extent on the shadowy presence of their original. When Robert Lowell in our day, or Innokenty Annensky a few decades before him, took over foreign poems for their own purposes, what they achieved was a new and virtually independent poem. Very few readers would be in a position to compare all Lowell's imitations with the originals: he was drawing on Latin and Greek, French and Italian, German and Russian. The imitations that Annensky made were published among his own poems, and should be taken as continuous with them, appropriations rather than imitations. He scarcely attempted to bring over the foreign setting. These poems were like the Moscow cathedrals as Mandelstam saw them—of alien design, 'but with a Russian name and in a fur coat'.

If the only successful translation depends on this rare sympathy between two poets, the bulk of it will be fairly small. A 'translator-general' like the Elizabethan Philemon Holland may undertake a series of prose works whose character is broadly the same. But in poetry— despite the example of Dryden or Zhukovsky—I doubt whether the 'translator-general' has any place. Both Dryden and Zhukovsky advanced the technique of verse by their translations, and Zhukovsky interests mainly for that reason. But in both the translator's own voice

E

and manner are too apparent. Nor could it have been otherwise. The translations that do miraculously succeed —so far as we may speak of success in this matter—are privileged. That is to say, many things have conspired in their favour. Pasternak would appear to have caught the very tone and movement of the Georgian poet Titsian Tabidze. If so, this was perhaps made possible by his extreme liking for Tabidze as a man in certain ways profoundly akin to himself, by the fact that he knew Tabidze intimately, and that Tabidze could have given him a perfect Russian paraphrase of the poems on which to work. His translations of Georgian poets delighted Tabidze, who thought them wonderfully accurate and musically true—even though Pasternak had no Georgian.

Something of imitation, a controlled surrender to another poet's mode, is required from the translator. The poem he attempts must be a discovery to him, almost on a par with his own experience. He has to respect the pattern, coherence and texture of the original; to roughen his style or elevate it; to take the very movement he finds, rapid or faltering or unequal; most difficult of all, perhaps, to pitch his translation somewhere between the two literatures, so that it is neither strange nor familiar. In so doing an excellent translator may add a new potentiality to the mother tongue. He will have pushed the frontiers of perception a little farther out for his countrymen, by setting the language to other tasks, and by showing the procedures that have been used elsewhere to convey particular states of mind, unexpected insights and unaccustomed feelings. There is a sense in which the world's literature may be seen as the collaboration through the ages of all writers, near and far, in developing their common expressive means. This goes on through the encounters of translation, as consciousness is slowly widened, and one language insists on being able to do what has already been done by another. In this way the vernaculars of Europe from the thirteenth century onwards gained power and flexibility by competition with the learned medium of Latin. And in this way more primitive languages all over the world school themselves by application to those that are more advanced.

It has seemed right to consider translation at this length because comparative study meets it so often. Translation is an instrument, however fallible, without which vast areas of the world's literature would be lost to us. It generally disappoints, it has small hope of durability, and yet as it falls back into the soil, progressively the soil is enriched. We have to treat every translation with wariness, knowing how much of it is a makeshift, an enforced compromise. The better we know our own literature, and have proved the capacities of our own language, the surer will be the instinct we acquire for judging a translation out of an unknown tongue. Where the English is sensitive and exploratory, we may have some confidence in the translator. To this it might be objected that the English of Ezra Pound is highly sensitive and exploratory, yet few translators have plunged more wildly than he. On the other hand, whatever his liberties and gross errors in detail, Pound has always shown a fine perception of the poetic qualities he attempts to render. Those who lack even the rudiments of Old English may yet grasp something essential about Old English poetry by carefully reading Pound's 'Seafarer', a faulty but inspired version. Dryden got to the heart of the matter when he said:

a Man shou'd be a nice Critick in his Mother Tongue, before he attempts to Translate a foreign Language. Neither is it sufficient, that he be able to Judge of Words and Stile; but he must be a Master of them too: He must perfectly understand his Authors Tongue, and absolutely command his own: so that, to be a thorow Translator, he must be a thorow Poet (1926, i.254).

In one area the thorough translator is more needed than ever before. The study of Greek and Latin literature has ceased to be general, at a time when interest in these literatures and their civilization runs very high. Thousands of people have read the *Iliad* and the *Odyssey* in the Penguin prose translations by E. V. Rieu, and the *Aeneid* in the verse rendering by C. Day Lewis. Very few of them will go on to learn Greek or to augment the little Latin they have. It seems that the literate person of our time will normally read the Classics in translation. But so, it may be urged, did Shakespeare. There are differences, though. Shakespeare, like other Elizabethan schoolboys, must have been well grounded in Latin. His use of the Latin element in our vocabulary shows that he understood the language and could draw out its less obvious meanings. And even if later he turned to Golding for his Ovid, and to North for his Plutarch, it must be remembered that classical learning was in the air. Ben Jonson, a popular playwright, loved to advertise it. The reader today comes upon a stale residuum of that influence here and there, in a leading article or an official report. The presence of Latin and Greek, the continual colloquy with the past—these are gone. It would be hard for a modern dramatist to conceive an imaginative sense of Rome at all like Shakespeare's.

For continuity with the Europe of yesterday the Classics must not be allowed to fall silent. The difficulties of translating them are worse than a century ago, before alienation had set in. We stand at a long remove from the classical world, in the condition of our lives, in our culture, and consequently in our language. 'Humane letters' is now a very old-fashioned phrase; urbanity no longer commends itself; the dignity of former ages too often looks preposterous. So the translator feels embarrassed when he has to mediate the tone of classical literature. Day Lewis's Virgil lacks neither force nor feeling. But too often the dread of formality unnerves his hand. Ours is a desperately self-conscious age when perhaps the major talent alone dare hope for that impersonal strength every good writer needs—and every translator.

Yet compared with some literatures—certainly with those from outside Europe—the Classics should be easy to communicate. Our language has many threads of connection with them; their essential tone so often occurs in our older literature. If they are unworthily translated, the loss will be brought home to the English language. The less it achieves, the more visibly its resources are shrunk. The translator's work has many disadvantages, but it holds together the body of world literature, and helps to keep language alive and supple.

5

Comparative studies at the university

How is the comparative sense to be fostered and put to use in the disciplined study of literature at the university?

A little ought first to be said about the nature and scope of a literary education. It would help to recall what Vico in the *Scienza Nuova* meant by 'philology' —the study of 'all that depends on the human will': the languages and the literature of mankind, the history and the customs. This was the ideal of philology as German scholars understood it, and there are signs that a similar outlook is returning today. The study of literature is increasingly bracketed with that of philosophy and history. It has always been difficult to set precise limits round the subject, and more and more other disciplines have thrown their shadow across literary studies. To interpret the great works of the past, or for that matter of the present, the most multifarious knowledge will be required. Nearly all the subjects taught in a faculty of arts will be laid at some time under contribution. The ideal critic should know where to look for enlightenment from theology, political theory, alchemy, depth psychology, the history of architecture and the visual arts, philosophy, aesthetics, folklore, the history of oral tradition and of typography. There are no bounds to this study, and new methods of illumination are constantly being found.

However, it will serve here to restrict the view and consider the study of literature in the first place as a discipline on its own, to which other interests may add something, but on which they are not permitted to encroach very far. The universities today, when they teach literature as a separate discipline, offer the choice between a single school that deals with one literature, or a comparative school that brings two or more literatures together, usually with the purpose of contrasting also the culture and history expressed through them. I propose to consider first the place of comparative study in the single undergraduate school, and afterwards the way it will function in a school deliberately planned to make it possible. Subsequently in the chapter I shall have something to say about comparative work at the graduate level, both in the form of a specially designed course and in that of individual research. And finally I wish to offer a few observations on the tasks before comparative study as a whole, not in the university context alone, but with an eye on the general development of literature.

(a) The Undergraduate Single School

Here the prime example is a school of English. Classics cannot strictly be termed a single school, embodying as it does two literatures; and generally in modern language schools two literatures are studied, though one may be taken in more depth than the other. Both classics and modern languages abound in opportunities for comparative work (even if these are not always acted upon). But a school of English sets out to be complete in itself. It may, as in many British universities, hold a balance however awkwardly between medieval and modern interests, philology (in the more restricted sense) and criticism (in the more expansive). There are those who, like W. W. Robson in his F. R. Leavis Lecture of 1965, contend that even without its earlier components (before the fourteenth century) such a school can provide 'a genuine body of knowledge'. This is the argument of Leavis himself, and it has many supporters. They believe that English studies can be made central and humanizing. Mr. Robson points out the inescapable weakness in many composite schools, which draw on a number of extraneous disciplines. Their effect, he says, will be that the student becomes 'too dependent on his teachers and lecturers; finding in his subject-matter no self-evident principles of order, he is debarred by the vastness of his inevitable ignorance from working out one of his own' (1965, 14). So he loses the chance of confronting his teacher, if temporarily, as an equal in at least one area.

The point is valid and it needs to be considered not only for composite schools, but for those which make free use of comparative study involving several literatures, or parts of several literatures, none of which allow very profound knowledge. However, I choose to defer it until we come to such schools in the following section. For the moment we have to examine the claim of English to present 'a genuine body of knowledge'.

Unquestionably we are dealing with a literature of great amplitude and power—a literature that would be remarkable if only because it includes Shakespeare. But is any one literature adequate to the end of providing, in itself, a true education? We are bound to admit that some parts of the European experience hardly entered into English literature; bound to tell our students that certain kinds of writing were better done elsewhere, and that some English authors demand the fuller perspective of Western literature to be understood and rightly evaluated. This becomes clear enough as soon as we reach our own period. It shows in the compendium by Karl Shapiro—*Prose Keys to Modern Poetry*. A glance through the chronological guide at the end reveals how many of the books and events that shaped the modern movement lie outside England and America. The same is true of the modern novel or drama.

Thus an element of comparative study would seem requisite even in a single school. It needs to form standards by reference to the best work in other literatures; otherwise it will always be open to the dangers of a complacent provincialism. The biggest gap to fill, and one increasingly common today, is an ignorance about classi-. cal antiquity and the Bible. Earlier centuries took a wide knowledge of both for granted. Without an ear for scriptural echoes in English writing, down to the time of Wordsworth and George Eliot and even of Lawrence, we shall lose many significant overtones. The Bible is not part of general reading in this age; but the student who lacks an idea of the Hebraic imagination, as mediated by the English Bible, can scarcely hope to comprehend the character of much seventeenth-century writing, for instance, or to appreciate the full resonance of Johnson. And equally indispensable is an acquaintance, even at second hand, with the classical tradition.

A freshman may bring up to the university some knowledge of Latin authors, though this may be sketchy and cut off from his English reading. It is imperative that he should learn, in however general terms, what the Latin background has meant to English literature, whether of the Middle Ages, the Renaissance, or the earlier modern age. Chiefly in his study of the Renaissance he will need to mobilize what Latin he has, and this should be supplemented by reading in translation (Golding's Ovid, North's Plutarch). There are so many notes in classical literature that he will want to distinguish, the better to hear English poetry. Dryden's magnificent version of Horace, *Odes*, III, xxix, *Tyrrhena regum progenies* (to be found among other translations and imitations in *The Oxford Book of Latin Verse*) probably gives as close an idea of the Horatian sensibility as you can find in English form. Those who have lost their Latin should read this poem and others like it (Dryden's rendering of the great conclusion to the second Georgic is also in *The Oxford Book*) and to that extent steep their imagination in Latinity. The account Gibbon has left of Roman peace under the Antonines; Milton's *Tractate of Education*, and his review of classical culture in *Paradise Regained*, Book Four— these clues and intimations should be known to the student, if only to tell him what was the air Milton and his contemporaries breathed. It will be far more satisfactory, of course, when he can lay a Latin text beside an English imitation—Juvenal's Tenth Satire to enhance *The Vanity of Human Wishes* or the satires and epistles of Horace to show the tact and the originality of Pope's imitations. (And there is good reason also for the student in a classical school to know about these English derivatives. They signify a conquest for his own literature of experience hitherto unappropriated.)

What limits are we to set on the supplementary knowledge that a student of English ought to acquire? He should ideally, if he is reading Old and Middle English as part of his course, know something about the heroic poetry of *Germania*, about the French medieval romance, about Dante and Boccaccio. Far more crowds into the picture with the Renaissance and the age following it; more still when we come to the nineteenth and twentieth centuries, and find that first German and then Scandinavian, Russian and American literature have to be reckoned with. The student is forced out of his own literature merely to understand it. And yet the English course alone reels under the weight of essential reading. Is there any guiding rule to be suggested here?

We might distinguish between two criteria. One is concerned with knowledge, the other with judgment—not that these two can be separated in any purposeful reading. However, it must be owned that the undergraduate often needs to ascertain facts which he then holds virtually in suspension. The Bower of Bliss in Spenser's *Faerie Queene* derives from the enchanted gardens of Armida in Tasso's *Gerusalemme liberata*. He notes the fact, and may produce it in an examination. The knowledge remains inert for him, particularly if he has small Italian. He may, of course, look up the passage in Fairfax's translation. After reading C. S. Lewis's *Allegory of Love* or Graham Hough's *Preface to 'The Fairie Queene'*, he should see more clearly the relevance of his information; but like a thousand other facts that he will accumulate as he goes along it adds to his knowledge but most probably does not affect his judgment. He hasn't the time to explore Tasso.

Take now a contrary instance. No student of the Middle Ages—indeed, no student of literature from any period—ought to neglect Dante. Without some experience of Dante we shall fail to conceive all that poetry can accomplish at the service of an ordered imagination. Nor shall we have formed a standard of excellence by which to judge other medieval poetry—Chaucer's, for example. Even if the undergraduate reads little more than the fine essay by Eliot, with its emphasis on 'the lucidity and universality' of Dante, he will at least have grasped the essential point: that Dante above all poets from his day to the present holds a central position in Europe. He links the Roman past with Christendom, and carried both forward into the modern age. Here then is one author whose presence cannot be overlooked. The English course that allows for some study of Dante, to be examined perhaps in a Finals paper, has clear advantages.

Almost as much can be said for Cervantes and Goethe, Tolstoy and Dostoevsky. Without a fair understanding of the last two, the student cannot finally assess George Eliot and Dickens. He ought to have read at least part of *Don Quixote* so that he may enter more clearsightedly upon the tradition of Fielding and the early Dickens (and Gogol). He should be able to put the first part of Goethe's *Faust* beside Marlowe's *Doctor Faustus* if only to reveal the gulf between the English Renaissance and the European Englightenment of the following age. Matthew Arnold will point him assiduously to Goethe, the 'genuine man' for Carlyle and so many other nineteenth-century admirers.

I realize that the distinction between knowledge and judgment is highly suspect. One would like to amass little knowledge that does not conduce directly to judgment. The chief aim in a school of literature should always be to make every reference a living fact for the imagination. But inevitably, when time is short and the syllabus nearly always too long, some information has to be noted and stored by for future use.

It emerges, I hope, from the argument so far that English literature, even when studied alone, needs amplifying. The English syllabus that can find room for one course on foreign literature, even if it has to omit some period or aspect of its own proper concern, appears to me better balanced and more satisfying. It comes nearer to providing 'a genuine body of knowledge'. We should not forget the complaints that Arnold allowed himself about the provincialism to be detected in our literature of the eighteenth and nineteenth centuries. It is also worth debating what Pound had to say about Chaucer, that he participated more fully in a general European culture than Shakespeare did (Pound, 1961, pp. 100–1). English alone will never fulfil the purpose that was said to be realized by classical studies, that of providing a central discipline of letters which carried in itself a complete civilization.

The single school, then, cannot refuse some aid from comparative studies. The limits within which they must work are evident. Comparisons will be brought in to illuminate English literature. Not only do they widen the perspective; they show more clearly what is characteristic and valuable in English writing. The justification of a single school is that, by centring on the one literature, it accustoms the mind to continuity. In a time of unpredictable change like the present, there is everything to be said for striking roots deep into a native tradition. Indeed, without this as the preliminary step, it seems doubtful whether comparative study can attain to its full value. Ideally one would wish every student to begin with the exploration of his own literature, and then, perhaps in a fourth year, to proceed to a comparative course. That should indubitably form the sequel, though at present, when three years alone are given to a first-degree course, it will probably have to come in the shape of post-graduate study.

(b) Undergraduate Comparative Studies

Most of the new universities in Britain have sought to break down the existing barriers between subjects. They propose 'Atlantic Studies' or 'European Studies', in which the attempt is made to reach the civilization behind a given literature or literatures, and in which history, philosophy and sociology are, to varying depth, made part of the course. Or they have set up schools of comparative studies at the undergraduate level, again with some attention to the different societies that have moulded each its own literature. The aim is reasonable. For too long the teaching both of English and of modern languages has sealed itself off, incommunicado and unconcerned. All too slowly the acquisitions of one discipline penetrate to another. There is only a faint recognition that literature transcends national boundaries, and that the study of it should be a common enterprise in which all the departments have to learn from and instruct each other. In the new universities it is customary for the divisions to disappear. Schools of literature replace the separate and unco-ordinated departments.

The advantages scarcely need pointing out. A well-designed school of literature will show a coherence, a sense of direction, a uniformity of critical standards which ensure that every part of its course can be given a heightened relevance to the whole. Under the old system, teachers of classics or modern languages have sometimes remarked that students of English taking their subject as a subsidiary bring to it a critical awareness which their own students may lack. In a school of literature this awareness becomes (or should become) general. We have to assume that English literature will form one of the subjects to be studied, not because critical thinking is in any way the monopoly of those who teach English, but for the indisputable reason that foreign literatures cannot be truly appreciated until you have some familiarity with your own. This was understood by the master who taught Coleridge and his schoolfellows to discriminate between classical authors 'on grounds of plain sense and universal logic'. But it might have remained an abstract discipline had not the boys been sent back to their native literature for a living comparison: 'At the same time that we were studying the Greek Tragic Poets, he made us read Shakespeare and Milton as lessons: and they were the lessons too, which required most time and trouble to *bring up*, so as to escape his censure' (Coleridge, 1907, 4).* It should, I think, be axiomatic that comparative studies for the undergraduate must include our own literature as a major element.

The benefits of a wide and well-integrated course will no doubt bring certain disadvantages to offset them. In the eyes of its opponents such a course will appear to have attained breadth at the cost of profundity. They will argue that odd fragments of two literatures or more have been morticed into a contrived pattern. The traditional school, however, confining itself to one literature, explores that literature from beginning to end—at least theoretically, though in practice certain lacunae are bound to occur. As Mr. Robson has indicated, the school that draws on 'a plurality of specialisms in related fields'—and to some extent this will apply to comparative literature—incapacitates the student for genuinely free and self-initiated work. He depends overmuch on his teacher because there are too many things new to him and in need of explanation. He does not know how to orient himself; and therefore the experience of learning can be only a partial one.

Mr. Robson had in mind the 'composite schools' that combine a variety of disciplines. It may be answered for comparative studies that by and large they are engaged in the one business of evaluating literature, and that literature everywhere is the same and presents the same problems. But even so the core of his objection remains. A comparative school has to select, and to select drastically. It may very easily inherit some of the deficiencies that belong to the 'general' school, in which three or perhaps four subjects are taken simultaneously.

* Coleridge's italics.

The principal weakness of the general school, however, lies in the random collocations that come about. Very few subjects truly march together. But in a comparative school the design is, if anything, too conspicuous. It lends itself to over-neat patterning. Only within a fairly tight scheme will the various elements be brought to make sense.

The comparative school faces its main problem in the ignorance of the student. There would be less difficulty if he had received a very thorough education in literature before coming up—if, for example, he had read classics as widely as the scholarship set of a good sixth form sometimes can (or could before it was encumbered by A levels). He ought to have gained some familiarity with French or another modern language. And he should have been taught, like Coleridge, to relate the foreign work to its counterpart in English literature. Such a candidate rarely appears, but he is the best suited for comparative study, and could derive very real value from it.

However, the normal student will possess few of these skills. But he should have an active curiosity, which the nature of the course itself ought to engender; and he can quickly be led to form the comparative habit. In what ways can he be guarded against superficiality and presumption? I suggest two will best serve. He must develop a rather unusual understanding of what he is about; and he must practise translation.

To take the second point first. It is a familiar complaint that students of English—and even more perhaps of modern languages—never learn to write, or to write anything but critical essays in a set style. Alter the occasion; ask from them not a critical essay, but a statement on any other lines, and the result will probably be nothing but clichés. One great merit of the old classical training was that it demanded so much translation. There may have been an excessive concern with the writing of Greek and Latin prose and verse. But nobody could gainsay the benefits of translation from these languages into English. Translation is often the poet's discipline, by the practice of which he can discover hidden resources in his own language. It is the educator of any student who wants to write an exact and flexible English. Translation involves him from the start in literature as a participant —the reader also becomes a writer. And the comparative school ought to provide ample opportunity for exercising this art.

However, translation is to be recommended not only on those grounds. It will ensure that the student has properly confronted a foreign author. Some of the best criticism in our day arises from closely inspecting a key passage. This is harder, of course, with a foreign text; and particularly for the inexperienced student. But he should be accustomed to this difficult exploration from the moment he can spell out a stanza of Pushkin or Leopardi. Nothing incites the powers of appreciation more than rendering a few lines by a foreign master into your own tongue. The necessity will remain to read as widely as possible in the foreign literature. But the regular practice of translation will see to it that the encounters are not superficial. Unavoidably some of the reading will have to be done from English versions, if the language is unfamiliar and initially hard, like Russian. However, a few dozen pages mastered in depth allow the student to move outwards from a firm base. He should make it a rule to examine the heart of every work in its own language.

The other safeguard of due attention is the intellectual temper a school like this should produce. Where the student even at the outset finds himself faced with comparative questions, he will need to form a clear notion

F

of what this study involves. The mind should be braced to difficulty; and it must quickly learn the procedures of criticism, in order to deploy the knowledge it acquires and to perceive significant relations, whether between individual works or contrasted literatures.

There can be nothing haphazard in the design of a comparative course. It does not shape itself more or less inevitably, in the way that a course based on a single literature tends to. A certain frugality of means will distinguish it, requiring that every part must be made to yield full value. That this may result a keen critical sense—the ability to ask the right questions—must be encouraged from the start. We shall probably find the approach in a comparative course more purposeful, more self-conscious, than that prevalent in a traditional one-subject course. The student is called upon to show some of the qualities that one would expect from a postgraduate.

As to the design itself I can offer merely a few observations. It would appear essential—and this has already been noted—that English literature should form one of the main components. Most probably the medieval period will have to be left out. An excellent comparative course dealing with medieval Europe, or with Europe of the Renaissance, could certainly be devised; but one of these would most likely exclude the other, unless four years were allowed; and the omission of modern literature would unfortunately seem inevitable. Such a course is better suited in my view for those postgraduates who have already gained some familiarity with a single literature in all its periods. A comparative course for undergraduates would more profitably be centred on modern literature, perhaps with the Renaissance as one period, the nineteenth and twentieth centuries as the other; or perhaps advancing from the later seventeenth century into the present. It may simply juxtapose the literatures of two countries in the same period; or it may use a variety of approaches (for example, treating a single genre like epic or the novel or verse satire). Whatever the choice of subjects, the purpose will be to reveal at once the affinity and the uniqueness of the literatures compared. If the student does any detailed work—and surely he must to enter the subject fully—it should relate to large problems and representative authors. The interesting figure of the second rank, who may have his place in the single school, seems more likely to drop out, unless it can be argued that he is important for what masses behind him.

All undergraduate courses in literature, single or comparative, are torn between conflicting demands. They seek desperately to combine width and depth. The comparative course merely poses the problem in a more acute form. The way out of this difficulty, as I have suggested, is to involve the student immediately in the great issues. Let him be made aware of the questions that stand before criticism today. Once he has acquired curiosity and the alertness of mind to relate everything he reads to a growing critical insight, no part of the course will be wasted on him; and what lies beyond the course will increasingly show for him on the horizon.

(c) Postgraduate Study: the One-year Course

Two kinds of study are offered at the graduate stage: either the course lasting one year which resembles undergraduate work in the supervision it requires; or the project of independent study (research) for two years or more embodied in a thesis. The one-year course may include a short thesis; but primarily it consists of lectures and discussions, the main difference from undergraduate work being that the student is more expert and should have a better command of one or two foreign languages.

For students who have come up through the single school this course may provide their introduction to comparative study as an end in itself. The subject is bound to be restricted, in order to allow for a thorough inquiry. A great deal depends on the choice of a field or topic. I have already suggested that a medieval or Renaissance study on comparative lines might be appropriate at this level. It seems, however, hardly enough to prescribe a period or a genre without having very clearly in mind what is likely to be gained in addition to more detailed knowledge. Here, and for postgraduate study in general, we should turn to the advice of Auerbach. It was his conviction that the scholar must look for 'a characteristic found in the subject itself' (Auerbach, 1965, 19), rather than start off in pursuit of some abstract category. His investigation into the meaning of two terms that defined the seventeenth-century public in France, *la cour et la ville*, is well known and exemplary for our purpose. By seeking to characterize each of these entities he was able to account for the tone and temper of French literature in that age, and to reveal more distinctly its limitations. Thus he could expose the predicament of a preacher like Bossuet, who, when inveighing against *la gloire*, the false and un-Christian ethic of the court and the town, yet had to use the very style of the court and the town to do so (Auerbach, 1957, 346–7).

I suggest therefore that even in a brief one-year course the attempt should be made to clarify certain key problems. The student might hope to provide at least the beginnings of an answer. The alternative method, which turns him loose in, or guides him through, a particular field (a genre or a period), may indeed throw up questions of real significance. These, however, ought to hold the central place in an organized inquiry. The one-year course may too easily fail to distinguish itself from a mere fourth undergraduate year. It can avoid this by taking themes and problems for which an undergraduate would not have been prepared.

See the Appendix for a specimen one-year postgraduate course.

(d) Postgraduate Research

The first condition of success in the comparative field is also one of the hardest to satisfy. A comparison should be firmly based at either end: it requires a broad knowledge of two literatures and two societies, their different traditions and outlooks. Accordingly, the choice of topic will be more limited than might appear. A suitable topic should define its own boundaries or it will collapse from uncontrolled extension. We have to remember that the simplest act of confronting two writers involves at the same time a host of other confrontations. Every writer brings with him the evidences of *milieu* and spiritual descent. He cannot be simplified to ease the comparison.

Further, the link itself should be strong and evident. Perhaps the most rewarding comparisons are those that writers themselves have accepted or challenged their readers to make—those that spring from 'the shock of recognition', where one writer has become conscious that an affinity exists between another and himself. Henry James felt this about Turgenev, Pound felt it about Propertius, Pushkin about Byron. To explore 'influence' here leads quickly into situation, and the reason why the example of one author should mean so much at a particular time and place to another. These are matters of inquiry which have their own clear justification, and they can be circumscribed.

I am not proposing that comparative study should always or even preferably deal in separate confrontations. But it seems well for the emphasis, at the outset, to fall markedly on the specific. There have been notable practitioners of comparative study who, like Ernst Robert Curtius, made it their rule to begin with 'the most general concepts', and so work through to the interpretation of particulars. Curtius had his eye on the continuities. He followed up 'expressional constants'—figures, *topoi*, themes (Curtius, 1953, 228). The danger in this method —which Curtius did not entirely avoid—is that a catalogue of instances may result, as a *topos* is identified in twenty different uses, without enough care being taken to establish the nature of each separate use. The same difficulty arises with the brilliant investigation by Mario Praz into nineteenth-century decadence, *The Romantic Agony*. He was looking for 'certain states of mind and peculiarities of behaviour' (Praz, 1960, ix), and again with so many instances of erotic sensibility we begin to feel that individual contours are being blurred. This applies equally to the work of Northrop Frye, when, for example, he propounds 'archetypal criticism' and 'the theory of myths' (Frye, 1957, 131–239).

Caution must be exercised in handling schemes of any kind—whether they comprise the development of a myth or a genre, a symbol or a rhetorical figure. One should constantly keep in mind the significance of the particular use. Was the myth central to a writer's preoccupations, and for how long? Did the genre bind his work despotically, or had he the daring to transform or even to parody it? The recognition of genres, not least when you have to deal with a poet like Wordsworth in whose poetry their character is often modified, has an obvious bearing on comparative study. So has the recognition of myths —indeed, of any determinants from outside which help to impart structure to an individual work. But we should not forget that the imagination can enhance its powers through resisting. The encounter with a genre tradition or a myth seldom leads to a straightforward and predictable result, except when minor art is in question.

Auerbach warned against the preoccupation with general ideas, such as 'the romantic' or 'the baroque', 'the idea of destiny' and 'the concept of time' (Auerbach, 1965, 18). It is true that in the last chapter of *Mimesis* he does examine 'the concept of time', or more specifically its treatment by some modern authors. One might say that the subject has been forced on him by the texts he is considering. The process began with a perception which was reiterated by further examples. Auerbach never lost sight of the circumstances in which a work developed. Literature for him was a continuous drama with vital interplay between its episodes; and everything took on a fuller significance when viewed at its point of emergence in history.

Research even on a modest scale will be fruitful if it learns not to ignore the essential relations in which a subject is best revealed. It ought to show indisputable links. I find that Santayana's arresting and subtle essay, *Three Philosophical Poets*, tends to abstraction. The continuity he discerns between Lucretius, Dante and Goethe is there by implication in so far as they can be cited to illustrate three principal phases of European thought (Santayana, 1910, 12). But the poets enter into no necessary connection with one another—necessary, for example, like that between Dante and Virgil (rather than Lucretius). For the literary critic the relation between them though interesting is fairly remote.

There are very wide opportunities for effective research. Here it may suffice to indicate some of the areas in which useful and concentrated work can be done.

The first of these, and one of the most rewarding, is the study of translation. It can achieve various ends. Versions of the same poet from different epochs may be compared, to trace the alterations of sensibility; characteristic turns of one language may be distinguished from those of another, revealing the national temper and tradition expressed through each; or translation may help to modify our understanding, our critical estimate, of the original work; or we may look for significance in the changes of emphasis, the suppressions and additions a translator has allowed himself. This would seem to be one of the points of intersection between literatures where the essential genius of either is most clearly exposed.

A work like René Wellek's *History of Modern Criticism* should remind us that the comparative study of critics such as Arnold, Sainte-Beuve, Belinsky or De Sanctis can show differences of tone and attitude which reflect the cultural situation of each. So too with historians: Peter Geyl has written about the presentation of Napoleon by French and other historians, or about the approaches of French writers to the Revolution. There is plenty to be said on the characteristics of national historians in the nineteenth century; and particularly on the rhetoric they use and its motivations. A Macaulay or a Parkman, a Karamzin or a Klyuchevsky, belong to the story of their national cultures no less than the novelists or poets.

However, the most obvious field for study is that of the leading forms—epic, tragedy, comedy, lyric poetry, satire, the novel. I have suggested more than once that the most profitable work will take place where a clear connection—an affinity or dependence or perhaps the deliberate rejection of an example—can be proved to exist. It goes without saying that a comparison should have regard especially to language and form—otherwise there will ensue a flood of generalizations about attitudes, climates of opinion, the national genius, etc. The necessary control will arise from a close study of texts, so that the distinguishing marks between them can be clearly established. It is certainly possible to choose as the ground of comparison not a formal or thematic resemblance but a common emergency—the French or Russian Revolutions, the Spanish Civil War—and to ascertain how it has been represented by writers of different periods and nationalities. But even here the exploration is likely to lead back into formal questions, since a writer shapes (or merely receives) his perspective for seeing the new event through inherited forms, or the guidance of a tradition that inclines him to one form more than another, even though he may greatly modify this. The most important thing in comparative study is to be able to apprehend each separate example of a writer's work as an entity—to recognize its individual contours, tones, rhythms, internal structure. In every kind of criticism these matter, but nowhere so crucially as in comparative study, open as it is to distortion and misunderstanding.

Lastly, a research student needs to acquire the sense of his own place in history. He should relate, wherever possible, his immediate problems to a total situation. It now seems fitting to say a little more about that situation, and about several tasks that comparative study might take in hand.

(e) The Wider Perspective

We have to consider the lines on which literature may be expected to develop. On the one hand, the reciprocity between national literatures is constantly growing; and more and more a common fund is being built up on which writers in any language may draw. The masterpieces that have hitherto stayed the possession of one people are becoming available to the world. (As I write this, the advertisement has just appeared of a book which will enable the Western reader to know the greatest of all Arab poets, Al-Mutannabī (915-65), who 'has seldom been translated or discussed outside Arab countries'.) Whole continents are becoming articulate—South America yesterday, Africa today. On the other hand, the status of literature, its reception, conceivably its character, are changing. The new electronic media may eventually displace literature.

Nothing will be served here by speculation. The practical course for those who wish to preserve literature and to extend it is plain. We must ensure that the writer's imagination in what may be a less and less favourable *milieu* should find nutriment from the greatest variety of sources. Not only work from the past, but even more that which is emerging out of the most recent literatures, the late-comers for whom certain springs are still open, can fortify the creative mind. This means that a lot of discovery and interpretation will be required. If there is any substance in Arnold's belief, and 'a great critical effort' really must precede a period of imaginative renewal, one can see in what direction that effort should point. Literature does not subsist merely on itself; but it grows through the accumulation of procedures and the extension of awareness. The more accurately we can be informed about its achievements anywhere, the more likely are fresh achievements to follow.

The means have now been made available to communicate everything of value in the world's literature to those who are interested. The next fifty to 100 years may see the canon, the central living heritage, immeasurably broadened. Comparative study has much to do in the promotion of a more comprehensive awareness. I shall go on in the next chapter to consider one example of the changing perspective, as it affects ourselves particularly. (One could argue that a similar position arises in the Hispanic field.) And I shall make certain suggestions about the role of the English critic at this point of time.

6

American literature—
the special case

As denizens of the English language we are sure to culti-
vate one special awareness. English provides the medium
for various literatures, among which American more than
any other compels attention. Not very long ago the
American writer and reader used to betray a consciousness, often unwilling, of their own literature as an appen-
dage to ours. The implied reference to England and
Europe was continually felt in American writing. I have
said earlier that the comparative habit seems natural to
the American mind—taking in, as it does, not only
English literature, but those of at least half a dozen
European peoples, and reaching out farther today even
towards China, Japan and India. Its cultural situation has
made America the principal centre of comparative study.
And now that American thought, American style,
American attitudes flow ever more strongly into
our own civilization, the comparative sense, at least with
regard to America itself, is beginning to form here. The
English writer and reader in the present age can feel
everywhere this mighty presence, by no means entirely
welcome. The home stretches of our language, its most
sensitive and intimate areas, are being invaded: the
Englishness of English begins to capitulate. By now it has

become utterly impossible to ignore American writing, which more and more sets the pace and determines the direction in our literature. English poetry today owes much of its impulse to American example. Our social thinking derives increasingly from American patterns. A full appreciation of American literature in its strength and its weakness ought to be acquired by any intelligent man in this age, and by Englishmen most of all.

Here is an opportunity no less than an obligation. We are bound as participators in a common heritage (it is largely that) to know, interpret and judge American literature. It concerns the English writer and reader not only because the progress of America bears on so many issues affecting the whole world, but also because the language which educates our feelings and guides our thought is rocked with the American impact. We must recognize what is happening or immense changes will have come about in which we are involved as mere captive sensibilities. 'English ought to be kept up'—not as the only or the dominant voice in the concert (this was never desirable), but as an equal among all the new overseas variants of our language. American literature has to be understood or English literature will rapidly cease to count. A culture that ignores what is happening outside very soon goes provincial and fails.

Equally our special relationship—a reality in culture at least—confers a privilege. Not only does it allow the English reader a new dimension of thought and feeling which he can possess without inevitably being possessed by it. Also, and perhaps here is the substantial gain, it breaks down the self-sufficiency, the inveterate philistinism and conceit of the Englishman which so tried Matthew Arnold. This threatened to make our literature more insular in the mid-nineteenth century than it had been in the seventeenth. The opportunity goes with the danger. English literature in the coming decades might easily compromise too far with American trends. Or, rising to take the challenge, it could achieve a radical perception of its own nature, of the traditions that have moulded it and are still not beyond recall, and also of the divergent American tradition. This would be a service from which both these literatures within one literature could benefit.

The tendency of the American mind in imaginative writing is very different from that of the English. It often drives to extremes, with an impatient absolutism to be found in other literatures—in the French classical period, for example—but wanting in America the weight and stability of an acknowledged tradition. In most ways American urgency appears antagonistic to English restraint (itself a waning characteristic). Richard Chase a few years ago contrasted the 'practical sanity' and 'equability of judgment' proper to the Victorian novel with the 'alienation, contradiction and disorder' of its American counterpart (Chase, 1958, 2). He makes a perfectly sound distinction for the last century, and one which retains some of its value for the present time, though the English imagination is no longer so normative as he reported it to be. Still, on the longest view, even though English literature may be moving out of its old orbit, a clear difference has existed and perhaps will continue to do so. The English writer appears less at home with violence; his addiction to it seems to have been willed in order to catch up with the war-time experience of Europe. It does reflect an evil in city life, as all modern cities veer towards Chicago; but it also reflects something of an abstract idea: the human condition read in American terms.

The characteristics of American literature have been modified since Puritan times; but there is enough continuity in a great deal of American writing to make it half foreign to English expectations. On their side the Americans have come increasingly to feel that the pre-colonial phases of English literature do not belong directly to them. The very beat and cadence of American English has to be recognized as a new phenomenon. American speech demands its own measures. While American and English writing seem to converge, the course has changed, and American literature draws English after it.

Certainly by his undergraduate years the student will read modern American literature as something that speaks to him. Faulkner, Hemingway, Salinger, Saul Bellow or Malamud, the Beat poets—these and many more have probably come his way, perhaps even at school. When so many judgments on our own literature are already fami-liar to him before he reaches the university, it is with a sense of real enlargement that he turns to American literature. Here too orthodoxies will meet him; but they are not his native ones and may conflict with them. An exploration of American writing from Cooper to the present age, however perfunctory, sharpens his interest in our own writing of the same period. Thus he en-counters a living relationship between literatures; he can see what a tradition is and how it develops; he begins to catch tones in the language of English and American writers, and to understand the implications when we speak of a national genius. Most undergraduate courses in English literature are overcrowded, but there should be room for an initial study of American writers along with their English contemporaries in the modern period. Even if this amounts to little more than the introduction of Hawthorne, Melville and Twain into a course on the nineteenth-century novel, it will have shown the limita-tions and also the strength of Victorian writers. It suggests a new range of possibilities in the novel form. The student may find himself drawn more powerfully to Melville's 'poetry of disorder' than to the stabilities in his own tradition.

As for the most recent period, no course on modern English poetry could overlook the Americans—not only Pound and Eliot, whose mark is so evident on it, but also Frost, Wallace Stevens, William Carlos Williams, Lowell. The same holds with the novel of the twentieth century, and with criticism. To keep abreast of American developments is as important for the writer as for the scientist or the engineer.

The pattern of American literature over the three centuries in which it has struggled from small beginnings to world stature takes on almost a diagrammatic quality. The first Puritan century exposes in clear form the little society out of which modern America has grown. Already one can read there some of the portents. Perry Miller claims that in Jonathan Edwards, the inheritor and last defender of the faith, there is to be met far more than a great theologian. Miller unhesitatingly calls him 'one of America's five or six major artists'. No doubt Hawthorne, Melville and Emily Dickinson would figure alongside him, and what places them there is a profound affinity with Edwards. Their genius was formed in solitude and dissent; and (more strikingly with the last two) it pushes to the limits. It shows the same curious amalgam of daring and obliquity; it moves appalled in a hostile universe. These four stand up against the easy optimism which had started in Edwards's day and chose eventually for its prophet Emerson. In American literature as in American thought the contrasts are pointed. R. W. B. Lewis finds a natural drama in the contest between the adherents of past and future from 1820 to 1860, leading to the emergence of a third party, the ironists like the elder Henry James (Lewis, 1955, 1–10). Again, as in the Puritan century, everything can be focused with an almost painful distinctness. The argument works itself out in the course of two generations. Such a concentrated phase when all the issues are made clear can be matched in the Southern renaissance after the First World War. Allen Tate recognized it as 'the curious burst of intelligence that we get at a crossing of the ways' (1955, 319). This too is of short duration—two or three decades. Since the war, another such phase has opened in New York; possibly it represents the last European afterglow in American culture.

The comparative sense is continually roused to attention by singularities of the American scene. Even at the beginning we learn that New England is different from New York, and New York from Philadelphia. But the most thorough contrast, deeper than any between the frontier and the old settlements, is obviously that of the two erstwhile nations, North and South. To distinguish and then to relate these cultures, giving heed to the differences and the common elements in the background of each, calls for critical power. There must be exactness of definition, backed by a longer perspective than is commonly taken. In this field comparative study can exercise all its resources: the familiarity with tradition under various aspects, the use of reference to analogues in the past (never pursuing them too far), the instinct for discovering the real affinities and deepest allegiances. The claims of the South to resemble France rather than the North in its religious and social feeling, or its belief that it constituted a high aristocratic society, need to be proven against our own experience of French culture and of aristocracies in Europe. So questions about American culture and writing lead back to the matrix from which America came.

G

American studies are no less valuable because they improve our ideas about European literature. The American conscience puts every reader on the alert with its searching and not easily answerable questions—the catechism that arises from a straight view of American culture. These questions touch ourselves very nearly, as Europeans and also as English people half-implicated in the history of the United States. We cannot treat them in isolation. They compel us to form that larger view which contains the single instance—America—and the setting in which to interpret and judge it. With an intensity of concern unknown since the days of Belinsky and his successors, American critics are scanning their literature for whatever light and leading it may impart. To read them is at once to be shaken out of assumptions about the prospects of society that not all English critics have challenged. Serious writing in America survives largely through the universities which train readers for it and subsidize many of the writers. This condition cannot be taken as wholly favourable to literature. In America the stresses in modern culture under the impact of technological change are exposed more brutally. They warn us to watch the signs over here. What befalls American culture will rebound upon us; the setbacks and recoveries have to be studied if our culture is taking the same road.

The exemplary aspect of American literature need not be stressed further. We are concerned with it only under the comparative aspect, and here American literature opens a wide view. In 1867 Henry James wrote to a friend about the advantages of being born American: '...we can deal freely with forms of civilization not our own, can pick and choose and assimilate and in short (aesthetically &c.) claim our property wherever we find it'. These words anticipate Pound's quoted at the beginning of the first chapter. They point to the simple and familiar fact that American literature connects with much besides English literature—that it has looked eagerly towards Italian and French and German, to Spanish and to Russian masters. The notion is that as America has gathered many races together so it should reconcile and adapt to its own purposes all the varieties of European —and not only European—literary excellence. (In no other country have the poets made a more serious effort to learn from Dante, whose order and completeness mock the chaos and fragmentation of American experience.) Therefore American literature presses the student to form his own conception of the whole Western inheritance, and to invoke, as Eliot did, 'the mind of Europe' which must accommodate America.

It is unquestionably with 'the mind of Europe' that we should approach American literature. We must practise the 'binocular vision' of Tocqueville writing on democracy in America. The finest critics and scholars of the United States never indeed forget Europe. In trying to make clear the peculiarities of American tradition they turn constantly to European precedent. Given the excellence of their scholarship, with its incalculable resources and strenuous disciplines, what, one may well ask, has Europe to contribute? It can give what the exiles a quarter of a century ago gave—men like Erich Auerbach, Renato Poggioli, René Wellek, Jorge Guillén. They presented the idea of Western literature in all its diversity, a multiple record with far more accumulated wisdom than is attained by any one tradition. There must inevitably be a risk that American studies will look inward, and that merely local estimates will prevail. When Matthew Arnold delivered his ungracious though salutary lecture on Emerson to American audiences, he showed them uncompromisingly how Emerson appeared in the light of nineteenth-century Western literature as a whole.

Arnold compared him with Newman, Carlyle and Goethe, but went on to speak of the defects in his poetry, his prose writing, and his thought. Emerson, despite all the important work he had done—'holding fast to happiness and hope' in a perplexed century—ought not to be admired for the wrong things. Arnold reinstates him at the end as a moral presence, like Marcus Aurelius, 'the friend and aider of those who would live in the spirit'. Today that moral presence seems very remote. The strictures Arnold made on Emerson's literary work have outlasted his rather sentimental praise of 'the hopeful, serene, beautiful temper'. What Arnold wrote on Emerson might be remembered now when too many authors are taken simply on their American rating.

The English critic has no commission to appear on American soil warning against provincial judgments. These are made no less freely here about English literature. But he does seem to be fitted for one serious task. American scholars have defined persuasively an American tradition in poetry and the novel. We understand the singularities of the American 'romance' form in fiction; we see clearly enough that 'all American poetry', as one critic has said, amounts to 'a series of arguments with Whitman' (Pearce, 1961, 57). The bias that shapes a tradition in these two forms being known, we shall not mistake American poetry in its characteristic tendency: it has gained recognition as a form that developed from certain impulses and against certain pressures. But to free it from misleading associations is no more than the first step. The American novel requires to be placed in a wider relation with the European novel as this developed in various countries; and American poetry, having been articulated in its own tradition, must now find its true alignment with the poetry of Europe. Wallace Stevens may have been right when he protested: 'Nothing could be more inappropriate to American literature than its English source since the Americans are not British in sensibility.' Nor are they European in sensibility, although their literature has manifold European sources. They stand half in and half out of English literature; their attitude towards Europe is compounded of piety and distrust.

Such an attitude, with the same antagonisms and the same moods of eager identification, has long characterized the Russians. We shall be able to judge American literature in a much clearer perspective by noting its resemblances to Russian literature, and also the contrasts. That the two literatures have a good deal in common is no discovery. Fifty years ago Lawrence found it natural at the outset of his *Studies in Classic American Literature* to cite Russian literature as near to American in feeling or 'pitch of consciousness'. Only their expression was very different. He set American subterfuge against Russian explicitness; but both bodies of literature had 'come to a real verge'—one that the European mind, however extreme it might try to be, could not attain (Lawrence, 1951, 8). Russian literature has not, of course, grown up inside a language already containing a much vaster literature; its medieval antecedents are native and continuity has not been snapped. But the relation it bears to modern European literature, from the early eighteenth century onward, is not at all unlike that of American. These two literatures move away from Europe into their own experiences, in part similar, in part so different. The confrontation between them, when examined in detail, brings out new aspects of each. Hawthorne and Gogol or Melville and Dostoevsky compare closely at some points, particularly when it comes to the deeper levels of apprehension. American seriousness ought to be distinguished from Russian. Both, however, issue in the same

kind of disturbing questions. The two literatures are alike
in their willingness to expose, even if the American hides
from the consequences in ambiguity.

The English critic should be able to interpret these
two literatures for their mutual benefit. With the Americans we share a language and in part a literature. With
the Russians we share less definable things—the experience of having emerged from medieval Christendom,
though its Latin and Orthodox manifestations differed;
an involvement in the general life of Europe, its wars
and interchange; most of all, the sense of a long national
past, of deep-seated customary forms in feeling and
thought, and of intimacy with an habitual landscape.
The Russian sensibility, however foreign its modes and
accent may seem, takes a familiar pattern; we have not
to unlearn anything of our own past in order to understand. As yet, the relating of these two literatures has
hardly begun. A fuller investigation would reveal more
about Western literature as a whole, and it might clarify
the lines on which to examine world literature.

Roy Harvey Pearce, after describing the continuity that
is to be found in American poetry, comes to the conclusion that perhaps 'there will be no American poetry
in the next half-century, that it will be a new international poetry' (1961, 433). This prediction is no more
than guesswork, but it seems warranted by the course of
American literature, which tends almost feverishly to ex-
pansion. Thus we are faced with a problem that has been
implicit throughout this inquiry. How and in what form
will the world literature announced by Goethe come into
being? He thought of an eventual fusion between literatures, a concert of all the separate national voices. There
is no likelihood that these will diminish in number. At
the same time a new form of supra-national consciousness is beginning to grow. In our epoch translation

flourishes on a scale never before known: the best things in the world's literature, or the most assimilable, are quickly spread about through translation into a score of tongues. This activity has been at its height in America, which contains a sample of most European communities. As a result American English has taken into itself much of the world's literature, and works once admitted in translation begin gradually to affect the bloodstream. I do not suggest that world literature will ultimately realize itself in American English. But possibly American literature, or rather the common literature of all peoples writing the English language, will provide one approximation to world literature. Four or five languages are likely to perform the same function, of serving as the equivalent of medieval Latin to a group of national communities. At present, for various reasons, the English language more than any other achieves this end. Thus the study of American literature, as dominant partner in that language, would seem to prepare us for the reception of world literature.

Bibliography

(a) Books referred to in the Text

ARNOLD, M. (1889), *Discourses in America*, Macmillan.
—— (1865), *Essays in Criticism*, Macmillan.
—— (1888), *Essays in Criticism*, Second Series, Macmillan.
—— (1960), *On the Classical Tradition*, ed. R. H. Super, Ann Arbor: University of Michigan Press.
AUERBACH, E. (1957), *Mimesis*, tr. Willard Trask, New York: Doubleday Anchor Books; 1st English edn., 1953.
—— (1965), *Literary Language and Its Public in Late Latin Antiquity and in the Middle Ages*, tr. R. Manheim, Routledge & Kegan Paul.
BAILEY, C. (1935), *Religion in Virgil*, Oxford University Press.
BARFIELD, O. (1952), *Poetic Diction: a Study in Meaning*, Faber: 1st edn., 1928.
CHASE, R. (1958), *The American Novel and Its Tradition*, Bell.
CLIFFORD, J. L., ed. (1959), *Eighteenth-Century English Literature: Modern Essays in Criticism*, New York: Oxford University Press.
COLERIDGE, S. T. (1907), *Biographia Literaria*, ed. J. Shawcross, Oxford: Clarendon Press.
CURTIUS, E. R. (1953), *European Literature and the Latin Middle Ages*, Routledge & Kegan Paul.
DRYDEN, J. (1926), *Essays*, ed. W. P. Ker, 2 vols., Oxford: Clarendon Press.

DUPEE, F. W., ed. (1947), *The Question of Henry James*, Allan Wingate.

ELIOT, T. S. (1965), *Dante*, Faber; 1st edn., 1930.

—— (1951), *Selected Essays*, Faber; 1st edn., 1932.

—— (1960), *The Sacred Wood*, Methuen; 1st edn., 1920.

FORSTER, E. M. (1924), *A Passage to India*, Arnold.

FRYE, N. (1957), *Anatomy of Criticism: Four Essays*, New Jersey: Princeton University Press.

HOUGH, G. (1962), *A Preface to 'The Faerie Queene'*, Duckworth.

HOWARTH, H. (1965), *Notes on Some Figures Behind T. S. Eliot*, Chatto & Windus.

JAMES, H. (1956), *Autobiography*, ed. F. W. Dupee, W. H. Allen. —— (1879), *Hawthorne*, Macmillan.

JOYCE, J. (1963), *A Portrait of the Artist as a Young Man*, Penguin Books; 1st edn., 1916.

LAWRENCE, D. H. (1955), *Selected Literary Criticism*, ed. A. Beal, Heinemann.

—— (1951), *Studies in Classic American Literature*, New York: Doubleday Anchor Books; 1st edn., 1923.

LEWIS, C. S. (1938), *The Allegory of Love*, Oxford University Press.

LEWIS, R. W. B. (1955), *The American Adam: Innocence, Tragedy and Tradition in the Nineteenth Century*, Illinois: University of Chicago Press.

MINER, E. (1958), *The Japanese Tradition in British and American Literature*, New Jersey: Princeton University Press.

MURRY, J. M. (1931), *Countries of the Mind*, Oxford University Press; 1st edn., 1922.

PASTERNAK, B. (1958), *Doctor Zhivago*, tr. M. Harari and M. Hayward, Collins and Harvill Press.

PEARCE, R. H. (1961), *The Continuity of American Poetry*, New Jersey: Princeton University Press.

POUND, E. (1961), *ABC of Reading*, Faber & Faber.

—— (1954), *Literary Essays*, ed. T. S. Eliot, Faber & Faber.

PRAZ, M. (1960), *The Romantic Agony*, tr. A. Davidson, Collins (1933, O.U.P.).

ROBSON, W. W. (1965), *English as a University Subject*, Cambridge University Press.

SANTAYANA, G. (1910), *Three Philosophical Poets: Lucretius, Dante, Goethe*, New York: Doubleday Anchor (reprint).

SEWALL, R. B., ed. (1963), *Emily Dickinson: a Collection of Critical Essays*, Englewood Cliffs, N.J.: Prentice Hall.

SHAPIRO, K., ed. (1962), *Prose Keys to Modern Poetry*, Evanston, Illinois: Row, Peterson & Co.

SPEIRS, J. (1962), *The Scots Literary Tradition: an Essay in Criticism*, Faber & Faber; first published, 1940.

STAPLES, H. B. (1962), *Robert Lowell: the First Twenty Years*, Faber & Faber.

STRICH, F. (1949), *Goethe and World Literature*, Routledge & Kegan Paul.

TATE, A. (1955), *The Man of Letters in the Modern World*, New York: Meridian Books.

TRILLING, L. (1966), *Beyond Culture: Essays on Literature and Learning*, Secker & Warburg.

YEATS, W. B. (1955), *Autobiographies*, Macmillan.

—— (1961). *Essays and Introductions*, Macmillan.

—— (1964), *Selected Prose*, ed. A. N. Jeffares, Macmillan.

(b) Further Reading

The nature of the subject is examined by René Wellek and Austin Warren in Chapter V of *Theory of Literature* (Penguin, 1963). Their Bibliography records a variety of statements on comparative literature, including that made by Fernand Baldensperger in the opening issue of *Revue de littérature comparée*, founded in 1921. Noteworthy in the list is Wellek's paper on 'The Crisis of Comparative Literature', delivered at the Second Congress of the International Comparative Literature Association (proceedings published under title *Comparative Literature*, ed. W. P. Friederich, Chapel Hill, N. Carolina: University of N. Carolina Press, 2 vols., 1959).

Werner P. Friederich and D. H. Malone have provided an *Outline of Comparative Literature from Dante Alighieri to*

Eugene O'Neill (University of North Carolina Press, 1954). There are a number of general reference books: J. T. Shipley's *Dictionary of World Literature: Criticism—Forms—Technique* (Routledge, 1943; 2nd edn., 1953); *The Columbia Dictionary of Modern European Literature*, ed. Horatio Smith (New York: Columbia University Press, 1947); and *Cassell's Encyclopaedia of Literature*, ed. S. H. Steinberg (Cassell, 2 vols., 1953). A. L. Guérard has written a *Preface to World Literature* (New York: Henry Holt and Co., 1940).

Two works on European criticism may be mentioned here: Wellek's *A History of Modern Criticism 1750–1950*, (New Haven: Yale University Press, Vols. I and II, 1955, Vols. III and IV, 1966; Cape); and *Literary Criticism: a Short History*, by W. K. Wimsatt and Cleanth Brooks (New York: Alfred A. Knopf, 1957), which goes back to Plato and Aristotle.

Besides *Revue de littérature comparée*, note should be made of the American journal *Comparative Literature* (founded 1949).

I have not discussed the study of oral literature, and referred very briefly to medieval studies. In both fields much comparative work has been done, e.g. *The Growth of Literature*, by H. M. and N. K. Chadwick (Cambridge University Press, 3 vols., 1932–40); C. M. Bowra's *Heroic Poetry* (Macmillan, 1952), written as a sequel to this; the much older but still current *Epic and Romance*, by W. P. Ker (Macmillan; first published, 1908); W. J. Entwistle's *European Balladry* (Oxford University Press, 1939); and, already listed, E. R. Curtius' *European Literature and the Latin Middle Ages*.

G. Highet's *The Classical Tradition* (Oxford University Press, 1949) details Greek and Roman influences on Western literature.

Most of what has so far been cited comes under the category of reference. The reader will want to see examples of comparative critical writing. Some have already been given in Section *(a)*. To these one may add: Benedetto Croce's *European Literature in the Nineteenth Century* (tr. D. Ainslie, Chapman & Hall, 1924)—separate studies, mainly of Italian and French authors; J. Middleton Murry's *Selected Criticism, 1916–1957*

(Oxford University Press, 1960); Thomas Mann's *Essays of Three Decades* (tr. H. T. Lowe-Porter, Secker & Warburg, n.d.). These writers show a European awareness comparable with Arnold's. But perhaps the ablest practitioner in the comparative field among working critics has been the American Edmund Wilson: (*Axel's Castle: a Study in the Imaginative Literature of 1870–1930* (Collins: Fontana, 1961; first published, 1931); *The Triple Thinkers* (Lehmann, 1952; first published, 1938); *The Wound and the Bow* (Methuen 1961; first published, 1941)). Quite as impressive in range but less penetrating is C. M. Bowra (*The Heritage of Symbolism*, 1943; *Inspiration and Poetry*, 1945; *The Creative Experiment*, 1949—all Macmillan). His book on the epic, *From Virgil to Milton*, was published by Macmillan in 1945. The reader is also referred in this connection to E. M. W. Tillyard's *The English Epic and Its Background* (Chatto & Windus, 1954). The late Renato Poggioli produced two excellent books of comparative essays (*The Phoenix and the Spider*, Cambridge, Mass.: Harvard University Press, 1957; *The Spirit of the Letter: Essays in European Literature*, Oxford University Press, 1966). Harry Levin has written two volumes which might be considered here: *Contexts of Criticism* (Harvard, 1957); *Refractions: Essays in Comparative Literature* (New York: Oxford University Press, 1966), though some of the pieces are disappointing. Wellek's *Concepts of Criticism* (Yale University Press, 1963) contains some masterly disquisitions on concepts like Romanticism, Realism, the Baroque.

The European novel has naturally proved a good subject for comparative work. In this area the Hungarian Marxist G. Lukács is particularly notable: *Studies in European Realism* (Hillway, 1950), *The Meaning of Contemporary Realism*, tr. J. and N. Mander, and *The Historical Novel*, tr. H. and S. Mitchell (both Merlin Press, 1962). See also Donald Davie's *The Heyday of Sir Walter Scott*, Routledge & Kegan Paul, 1961, which takes in Pushkin, Mickiewicz, some Irish writers, and Fenimore Cooper.

On translation the reader should certainly consult Arnold 'On Translating Homer' (see Section *(a)*). He might follow with E. S. Bates's *Intertraffic: Studies in Translation* and *On Transla-*

tion, ed. Reuben Brower (Oxford University Press, 1967). Stanley Burnshaw's *The Poem Itself* (Peregrine, 1966) gives the text of poems in half a dozen European languages, with a free version in prose and an appreciation of each.

Finally, I should like to note Leo Spitzer's *Linguistics and Literary History: Essays in Stylistics* (New Jersey: Princeton University Press): it has analyses of passages from *Don Quixote*, *Phèdre*, Diderot, Claudel. The road of stylistics, particularly in comparative study, is a difficult one; but Auerbach (see Section *(a)*) and Spitzer have shown that it leads to striking discoveries.

Appendix

Sketch of a One-year Postgraduate Course in Comparative Literature.

This course has been designed for students whose first degree was taken in either English or a modern language. It is assumed that the former category will have a good working knowledge of one foreign language and some acquaintance with its literature; and that the second category will have studied English either as a subsidiary or one-year additional subject. There are five elements in the course, which I have arranged in a three-term syllabus.

First Term

(a) Introduction to Comparative Method
This might be done largely through the examination of critical writings that bear on the topic of comparative literature, e.g. Auerbach's *Mimesis* (the final chapter); Baudelaire, '*Edgar Poe, sa vie et ses œuvres*'; Lawrence, chapters from *Studies in Classic American Literature*; Pound, 'The Serious Artist'; Eliot, 'What is a Classic?', etc.

(b) The Practice of Translation
Exercises in translating from the foreign language a candidate offers, accompanied by the reading of such commentaries on the translator's art as Arnold, 'On Translating Homer', and by the study of established translations against their originals.

(c) *Study of a Genre* (in English and one other literature)
This would deal with selected work in the genre (e.g. picaresque novel, realist novel, verse satire, Symbolist poetry), concentrating perhaps on two or three authors belonging to each literature.

Second Term

(a) *Study of a Special Problem* (as it arises in English and one other literature)
Problems that suggest themselves are, e.g., the critic and society (Arnold, Belinsky, Sainte-Beuve, De Sanctis); censorship, hidden or overt (as in the Victorian and the nineteenth-century Russian novel); 'verse as a dying technique'; urban sensibility (in, for example, Dickens, Baudelaire, T. S. Eliot, Blok); the poet and patronage (Dryden, Pope, Molière; Goethe, Zhukovsky, Pushkin).

(b) *The Practice of Translation* would continue throughout the second term. Likewise *(c) Genre Study*.

Third Term

The writing of a short thesis (10,000–15,000 words) on a limited topic from (b), (c) or (d).

It will be noted that the course demands a study of English literature as an equal component with the foreign literature chosen.

Topics such as the relations of literature to painting, music or philosophy are reserved for the next stage (M.Litt. or Ph.D.), where, if they are studied, it should be in connection with at least two literatures (not necessarily English among them).